BLUE TIGER

BY

KENNETH D. WILLIAMS

ISBN: 1-4033-9191-2 (e-book)
ISBN: 1-4033-9192-0 (Paperback)
ISBN: 1-4033-9193-9 (RocketBook)

Library of Congress Control Number: 2002095532

This book is printed on acid free paper.

Printed in the United States of America
Bloomington, IN

1stBooks - rev. 01/09/03

Chopper To Heaven

By Kenneth D. Williams

The Cavalry soldiers ran toward the waiting chopper.

None of them wanted to be left behind.

They ran as fast as they could with the enemy right on their tail.

The last soldier felt a pain in his back, and then another pain in his thigh.

He stumbled but kept running toward the chopper.

The chopper crew waved for them to hurry,

But the soldier fell behind the others.

He was still running as the others boarded.

The chopper started to rise without him.

The soldier reached up to the ascending chopper,

. . . And then God reached down . . .

And pulled the soldier into His chopper bound for heaven.

ACKNOWLEDGEMENTS

I give a lump in the throat thanks to my wife, Linda, and my sons, Leland and Scott, for standing by me when I was not worth standing by. A big thanks to my rough draft typist, Sheri, who had to decipher my sloppy handwriting. I thank my wife for typing the last rough draft. For the right direction my friend the Reverend Tracy <u>Wilson</u> gave me, I am indebted. To the person who suggested I write my story, Vet Center counselor, Chris Lujan, a special thanks. You were right, Chris, my burden became easier to bear with each word I wrote. For the encouragement and direction I have been given, I thank very much, fellow author John Erickson.

And to my Lord Jesus Christ, I am grateful for Your love that saved a sinner like me.

DEDICATION

I DEDICATE THIS BOOK TO ALL VIETNAM VETERANS, ESPECIALLY MY YOUNGER SISTER, PHYLLIS, A VIETNAM VETERAN WHO COURAGEOUSLY FOUGHT CANCER. AT FORTY EIGHT, SHE DIED TOO YOUNG.

TABLE OF CONTENTS

Ecclesiastes 3: 3 - A time to kill, and a time to heal; A time to break down, and a time to build up; The Holy Bible.

FOREWORD

As I sat and pondered what Chris Lujan, my Vet Center Counselor, had suggested to me in our last counseling session, I opened my Bible to Ecclesiastes, chapter 3, and read to myself. When I came to the third verse, the words bounced out AT me. I read the third verse over and over as my tears flowed like two streams down my cheeks. Chris had suggested that I read my Viet Nam diary and write about my combat experiences to facilitate my own healing from PTSD (Post Traumatic Stress Disorder.) This Book is a result of my healing process. First, I had to stop my alcohol abuse. Second, I had to look honestly at the hidden past. Twenty years after writing my diary (1967 - 1968), I picked it up for the first time and read it, and the memories came forth. This book contains many experiences out of twelve month's worth, but this writing helped me deal with my past and put the past in the past where it belonged. The more I read and wrote, the more I felt relieved from my depression, aggression, and hurt inside. This work was a true cleansing of my body, mind, and soul.

One of the first entries in my diary was in October, 1967. The troop ship, USNS General Walker, was our ride to Viet Nam. The evening we set sail out of San Francisco Bay, all of the troops aboard the ship were on deck watching the lights of Oakland and San Francisco disappear behind the horizon. There were over a thousand of us on deck, but it was so quiet that you could hear hearts beating. We all sat pondering possibly the same question. — Will I ever see home again? Nobody spoke or moved until we were well out to sea, and we could see no more lights on the darkened horizon.

The first words I heard came from my buddy, "Spider". He asked, "Bear, will you make me a promise?" I replied by nodding my head yes. Spider then asked, "If I don't make it back from Nam, will you make a point to see my folks and let them know the truth?"

"Yes, I will," I replied. Then I asked the same of Spider and he said he would do the same for me. I thank the Lord that neither one of us had to fulfill that promise.

I left a pregnant wife and a son at home while I was sent to fight another country's war. We all left something or someone behind as we headed straight toward eternity.

We were all young innocent men scared of the unknown future but bent on proving ourselves on the battlefields of Viet Nam, not knowing that this impending experience would change us forever.

Thank you Lord for my blessing of healing.

D TROOP 3rd SQUADRON 17th AIR CAVALRY REGIMENT

The 3/17 Air Cav was reactivated in November 1966 at Fort Knox, Kentucky. The previous Viet Nam era 3/17 Air Cav unit was absorbed by the newly formed 1st Air Cavalry Division and was redesignated the 1/9 Cavalry.

In Viet Nam, the 3/17 was assigned to the 1st Aviation Brigade and the 12th Aviation group. The 3/17 consisted of headquarters troop; three helicopter troops - A, B, C troops; D troop - the versatile ground troops; and F troop - the support group. Headquarters troop function was administrational and logistical support. A, B, and C troops consisted of helicopters such as scout choppers (LOH), Cobra gunships, slick choppers (UHI). An aero rifle platoon was assigned to each of the troops. F troop was the maintenance and other support groups unit and not really a troop as such.

D troop was a very versatile part of the squadron. First, the troop was a mounted unit consisting of jeeps and 3/4 ton trucks.

Each of the three platoons consisted of gun jeeps, 106 M M anti tank jeep, 81 M M mortar 3/4 ton truck, infantry 3/4 ton truck, and command jeeps all used for road clearing missions and convoy duty. Second, each platoon could be used as an air mobile infantry assault unit in a matter of minutes. Third, each platoon could be used as an infantry platoon doing perimeter guard duty, conducting sweeps of an area, ambush patrols, and fire base security. Fourth, each platoon could be used as a long range reconnaissance unit. Fifth, the troop could not only do all of the above as a troop force but could operate just as effectively as individual platoons or squads. Most of the time the three platoons were performing three different missions at the same time.

The 3/17 traveled to Viet Nam on the U.S.N.S. General Walker troop Ship in October 1967 with its sister unit the 7/17 and one other unit. After twenty three days at sea, the ship docked at Qui Nhon where the 7/17 disembarked. The troop ship continued South to Cam Ranh Bay to let off the other unit. The 3/17 landed at Vung Tau Southeast of Saigon and were transported to their main base camp at Di An. Although Di An

2

would always be their main base of operations, A, B, C, and D troops never spent much time there. The various troops were attached separately to other major units in different areas of operation and never really worked together as a squadron.

D troop, for instance, was on the move constantly from fire support bases to main bases performing the wide variety of missions for which they were trained. D troop's motto was "Go ahead on, Blue Tigers", and that is what they did all the time. D troop's call sign was Blue Tiger thus the title of this book.

While the rest of the troops wore the traditional cavalry stetson hats, D troop was awarded the maroon beret for their excellence in training against the Rangers at Camp Dohlonega, Georgia and the Special Forces at Camp Dawson, West Virginia.

D troop consisted of three platoons, and each platoon consisted of thirty six soldiers.

Each platoon was recognized by their radio call signs. The first platoon's call sign was Blue Tiger One plus a number to designate who was talking on the radio. For example, Blue Tiger One-Six would be the first platoon's platoon leader. The second platoon had the two plus numbers, and the third platoon had the three plus numbers. The single digit call signs were used by the troop commander and his Headquarters Group.

When the platoons were vehicle mounted, the platoons were organized as follows.

The scout gun jeeps were World War II model jeeps with a M-60 machine gun mounted in the back. There were three scout jeeps per platoon. The gun mount was high enough for the gunner to stand up in the back of the jeep and fire the mounted M-60 belt-fed machine gun. The scouts were often referred to as the Rat Patrol named after their World War II counterparts. The machine gun could swivel 360 degrees to shoot in all directions, or the gun could be kept stationary by placing a pin in the mount especially for traveling. Each scout jeep had three soldiers or scouts; one gunner, one driver, and one car commander who was usually a squad or section leader. Each jeep was equipped with a radio (PRC-25).

The command jeep for the platoon leader usually did not have a gunner. The jeep consisted of a driver, the platoon leader and two or three radios. One radio was tuned to the platoon radio frequency. One radio was tuned to the troop radio frequency.

And if there was a third radio, it would be tuned to the radio frequency of the unit the D troop platoon was assigned or a fire support unit.

There was one jeep with a 106 MM antitank gun mounted on it with a radio. Three men were assigned to the jeep: a gunner, a driver, and a car commander. Usually, all three were proficient at firing the 106 MM antitank gun.

The platoon sergeant had his own gun jeep armed and manned like the scout jeep.

The infantry squad rode in a 3/4 ton truck with a radio. The squad consisted of twelve men including the squad leader and the driver. The infantry squad was armed with a M-60 machine gun, M-79 grenade launchers, and M-16 rifles. The truck also carried the platoon's extra ammunition and supplies.

A medic was assigned to each platoon, and he usually rode in one of the 3/4 ton trucks.

At times though the medic rode in any empty seat that was available.

The 81MM mortar squad rode in a 3/4 ton truck with a radio and four soldiers who were trained mortar men including the driver and the squad leader. They were armed with M-16 rifles as well as the 81MM mortar and mortar rounds. The truck also carried the platoon's extra ammunition and supplies.

All of the vehicles' radios (PRC-25) could be taken off the vehicle and mounted to a backpack for dismounted missions.

All of the men in the platoon were cross-trained on every weapon in the platoon so that each man could fill any position in the platoon. This allowed the platoon to continue to operate when personnel were gone for some reason.

Technically that was how the three platoons were manned, but in a not-so-perfect world as in any war, the platoons were always under strength. The gun jeeps and 106 jeep were kept fully manned with the soldiers from the other squads filling in the missing positions.

When one of the platoons became an air mobile assault unit, a reaction force, or a stationary force (which they could become any of those in a matter of minutes), the platoon would consist of an infantry scout squad, two infantry squads, and the command post. Each of the scout and infantry squads would consist of ten to twelve men with the command post consisting of five men. The platoon leader, the platoon sergeant, the medic, and two RTOs made up the command post. One radio man (RTO) was tuned to the platoon frequency and the other RTO was tuned to a support frequency. But as was stated earlier, that would be in a perfect world. When the platoon went air mobile, the mortar men did not carry the 81MM mortar even though it was portable. The platoon relied on their own M-79 grenade launchers or air and artillery support for what the 81MM mortar usually provided.

Although the 3/17 Air Cav troops were very active in the war, in the Viet Nam history books a reader will find very little mention of the unit. Usually that mention was in relationship to another unit such as the 25th Infantry Division, the 1st Infantry

Division, the 9th Infantry Division, or the 101st Airborne Division.

The history of the 17th Cav goes all the way back to 1916 and continues today as the 3/17 is part of the 10th Mountain Division in Europe and Afghanistan. (See Addendum)

(A note here about Viet Nam veterans.)

Viet Nam veterans have taken the brunt of negative news reports and movies over the years so much that it is disheartening! Some Americans tend to believe those negative depictions of the Viet Nam veterans. Why do people want to believe that about fellow Americans? Viet Nam veterans were fathers and mothers, uncles and aunts, brothers and sisters, sons and daughters, and cousins. They were <u>not</u> monsters or killers.

They were scared but brave Americans. They made mistakes, but in the end they did that for which they were trained. They, after all, were only human. This book is based on true war experiences of D troop 3/17 Air Cav as best captured in a daily diary so many years ago. "Go Ahead On, Blue Tigers!"

OPERATION YELLOWSTONE - BAIT FOR THE TRAP

After arriving in Viet Nam the 3/17 continued intensive in - country training at Di An.

The training consisted of mounted and dismounted patrols, night ambushes, sweeps of areas, firing weapons and mortars, perimeter guard, and filling "millions and millions" of sand bags in their spare time in the boiling hot sun. The officers called it "becoming acclimatized". But the troops called it hard work among other things. D Troop was sent to fire support base Hanover with the 1st Infantry Division unit for four days and got their feet wet (so to speak) as what was to come. Perimeter security, sweeps, ambushes, and camping out in the jungle. The 3/17 had one man wounded on ambush patrol.

On December 7,1967 the unit as a whole was moved to a fire support base at Soui Da as part of Operation Yellowstone with the 25th Infantry Division. The fire base set on the East side of a large mountain which stuck up out of the flat land like a sore thumb.

It was named Nui Ba Den. The troops called it the Black Virgin Mountain.

The Special Forces had a communication base on top of Nui Ba Den. Delta troop's assignment was to secure and protect the perimeter, night ambush patrols, furnish listening posts for the base, daytime mounted and dismounted patrols, air mobile missions, and in their spare time — fill sand bags and build bunkers. The heat and humidity and insects were always a part of the day and night. It was the dry season when it seldom ever rained, and when the helicopters would land the dust was stirred up like a West Texas dirt devil. There were no shower facilities— the troops bathed out of their helmets.

There were no restroom facilities — just a shovel to cover it up. A lot of the meals were "C" rations (canned food in a box) although D troop had the best cooks in the Army and they could put on a great feed. Water was scarce but ice was even more so. Hot beer tasted better than hot cokes anyday.

D troop had many missions during this period, but most of them were without much action and just plain hard work. Work all day and work all night with a few hours rest here and there. A typical day would consist of; off guard duty, or ambush patrol at sun up, hump the boonies most of the day, rest a few hours, fill some sand bags and go out on ambush patrol or guard duty again that night. The sweltering heat and bugs just became part of life each day and night.

On several air mobile missions, Delta troop had discovered V C villages on their sweeps through the jungle. Several times no one was home but they had just left the area as campfires were still burning. It was an eerie feeling like when you feel someone is watching you but you can't see them. The troops would destroy all the hooches and bunkers and mount the choppers and go back to Soui Da base camp.

Bear was a dry flat land Panhandle of Texas soldier who had not grown up with humidity and the trees like he found in Kentucky, Georgia, West Virginia, and now Viet Nam.

Bear was in the 81 MM mortar squad (third platoon). On nights that he wasn't assigned to fire illumination rounds most of the night or fire missions if a ambush patrol needed it, he like the other mortar squad soldiers was just another grunt on guard duty or ambush patrol. This would be the only time for mortar squad duty because he was assigned to the scout squad shortly after Operation Yellowstone.

On December 30,1967 Delta troop was sent on an air mobile mission. Bear was the platoon leader's RTO on the platoon frequency. On a troop mission the platoon leader would have two RTO's - one on the platoon frequency and one on the troop commanders' frequency.

Bear had just gotten off perimeter guard duty a few hours earlier when the order came to mount the choppers for the air mobile mission. D troop loaded the waiting helicopters by platoons with a squad in each slick. The third platoon was the last to load up in the dusty air the choppers stirred up. Bear and the other grunts sat quietly on the floor of the chopper (as the slicks had not seats in them) each one thinking the same thing — will this be my last day. As was his ritual, Bear repeated the Lord's Prayer, and the 23rd Psalm silently as the choppers circled the LZ waiting for the gun ships to quit their attack on the LZ. The LZ was smoking from the gun ships' rockets. This was the first vulture flight D troop had been on although Bear had not heard that term used as yet. Bear slid out the door and put his feet on the landing rail holding on for dear life. As he was waiting to jump off, Bear watched the ground get closer and closer.

Then as the chopper pilot cut the power for an instant, Bear jumped to the ground a foot or so off of the ground. Bear barely hit the ground when the LT was hollering for him to move, move, move. Bear ran toward the wood line firing into the woods with his M - 16. Out of the woods straight ahead eight V C ran off to the left. They didn't get very far because a gunship mowed them down with its mini guns and rockets.

"Bear" the LT screamed "Call 34, (the infantry squad) and have them check out those VC".

"34 Delta this is 36 Delta over" - Bear called.

"This is 34 Delta, go ahead Bear".

"36 said for your squad to check out those VC the gunships shot".

"Roger Bear. We're already here. They're all dead. We're searching the bodies now." 34 Delta replied.

Bear relayed the message to the platoon leader. After which, all of the squad leaders met with the platoon leader and platoon sergeant. Each platoon had already secured their part of the LZ and waited for orders.

After a brief meeting, the leaders went back to their own men and the troop started to sweep in a circle around the LZ in the jungle. The scout squads were out front of each platoon cutting a path if need be through the thick underbrush. The first two platoons were on line making a wide sweep around the area with the third platoon working behind them to secure the command post (CP) and guard the rear of the unit on their sweep.

The troop ran into a small swampy area and trudged on through it knee deep in the nasty water. With ten minute breaks every 'thirty minutes it took forever to get around the outside of the LZ. Bear figured the troop must have walked a 1000 meters through the jungle with no more contact. The troop commander seemed to be in no hurry and it took about three hours to completely circle the LZ. By this time Bear was ready to drop. His clothes were soaking wet not only from the swamp but from the heat and humidity and the extra weight of the radio on his back. When the troop completed the sweep, the LZ was secured again and they waited to be picked up and flown back to Soui Da.

After awhile, Bear wondered where were the choppers. The troops waited for a long hour at least.

"Bear what's going on" - came over the radio.

"I don't know We're just sitting here", Bear replied.

Some other squad RTO spoke up - "Well we're going to get our butts kicked if we hang around here. We've made enough noise to wake the dead".

"Roger on that" Bear replied.

The lieutenant asked Bear what was going on.

"Nothing sir, everyone's just getting restless" Bear answered.

"Well, tell them to observe radio silence" LT said.

Bear repeated the order on the radio "Radio silence now".

It was silent.

After about ten minutes, a battle could be heard in the not too distant. The CP came alive and issued orders to get in position and secure the LZ for pick up.

The troop moved out into the LZ and each squad got ready to be picked up. Yes, the third platoon was the last in line to be picked up.

The distant battle seemed to get closer and louder Bear thought as he waited for the last slicks to come in to pick up the third platoon. In came the choppers – what a great sound when you know they are coming to pick you up.

Bear jumped at the chopper door and banged his knee going in. Man that hurt Bear thought as he turned around in the doorway. The chopper was already forty foot in the air. A grunt had better load up in a hurry or be left on the ground. As the chopper cleared the trees and banked toward home, Bear saw the battle below not too far away and wondered if Delta troop was used to draw the VC out into a battle.

Alas, bait for the trap!!

FIRE BASE BURKE

During the last days of January, 1968, the Tet Offensive occurred. This Tet Offensive was a huge push by the Viet Cong to retake base camps, villages, and even the larger cities, like Saigon, all over Viet Nam simultaneously. Tet is the Vietnamese New Year.

On January 7,1968, 3/17 abandoned their fire base at Soui Da, located on the east side of Nui Ba Den, which was called the "Black Virgin Mountain". It rose up out of the jungle out of nowhere it seemed. It must have been a giant volcano, long ago. The unit moved back into Tay Ninh base camp to give them more protection as they continued their missions in the Tay Ninh area. The scuttlebutt was that command was anticipating a major push of some kind by the Viet Cong during Tet. And if need be the 3/17 could help defend the base camp.

After all hell broke loose, D Troop was rushed to Soui Da on the 29th of January, to sweep and secure the Route 13 road and bridges all the way to Fire Base Burke. Their mission, after they

17

arrived at Fire Base Burke, was to provide perimeter security until the artillery unit and the 5th Mechanized Infantry Unit was ready to pull back to Tay Ninh. Then D Troop was to provide convoy security to Tay Ninh with their gun jeeps.

According to the artillery soldiers with whom the D Troopers talked, Fire Base Burke had been there only a short time, but the base had been overrun by the VC several times. Fire Base Burke was just literally scratched out of the jungle., as it was a forward artillery base. It was a ragged looking place encircled by concertina wire. The jungle came right up to the perimeter wire. There was very little clear fields of fire.

On the 29th of January, the third platoon was left at the bridge on the East side of Soui Da, to spend the night and secure the bridge until another unit could relieve them

The first and second platoons swept and secured the road to Fire Base Burke.

It was a hot, dusty afternoon when the third platoon got to the bridge East of Soui Da. They dug fox holes, filled sand bags, and rolled out concertina wire to give them some protection for the night. Just before dark, the troops set out claymore mines and set up fields of fire. It turned out to be a long night - watching and waiting. Sometime after midnight, Bear dozed off to sleep. Bear was awakened by the movements of one of his claymore mine triggering device being pulled out of his foxhole. He immediately grabbed for the trigger and pulled back on it until the trigger wire went limp. "Charlie was definitely around." Bear figured he dared not fire that claymore mine because "Charlie" may have turned the mine toward him in hopes that he would blow himself up; "Charlie" may have stolen the whole mine.

Bear stayed wide awake for the rest of the night. The next morning, Bear found the blasting cap pulled out of the mine, and the mine was lying on its back facing the sky. Bear figured that when he grabbed the trigger, he had scared "Charlie" off. Bear followed the VC trail for a short distance into the treeline, and put a trip flare across the path in case the VC came back. A LP (listening post) had been hit last night, and a KIA was dusted off to Tay Ninh, thus explaining the gunfire.

The third platoon was relieved of the bridge duty about noon, and they moved up to Fire Base Burke to join the rest of their troop on the perimeter. The feeling of imminent danger was thick in the air as they dug in and strengthened the perimeter. The artillery unit fired fire missions off and on all day. It was very hot, when the choppers flew in and out throughout the day, it was very dusty. Bear set his M - 60 machine gun field of fire. After supper, the ambush squads and LPs were notified and got ready to go out about dusk. Bear stayed in base camp, and thought to himself, "This is great! I might get some rest." Boy was he wrong! This would prove to be a terribly long, eventful night.

The long night began way before dusk. The VC played mind games with the Fire Base soldiers. The VC lit various small fires all around the perimeter, way out in the jungle. The fire would go out after a few minutes, and then as it got darker, the jungle became filled with eerie glowing lights from the embers. It was learned later that these were torches used to light the staging areas. The word passed quickly throughout the camp.

The devil was restless tonight. The 105 MM Howitzers lowered their gun barrels to ground level anticipating a ground attack. The howitzers were loaded with beehive rounds, which were rounds filled with thousands of small nail - like metal pieces. These rounds were made for ground attacks and could really tear up a body, jungle or anything else in the way.

As the LPs and ambush squads moved out of the perimeter toward their positions, everyone else watched with the same pained, worried look on their faces. They were thankful it was not them going out, but concerned for the buddies who were. Bear went to the Command Post and gathered some more M - 60 rounds which gave him over 1,000 rounds. He prepared his fighting position for the night. Bear was the only person at his position because the unit was strapped for men, especially since they had to put out LPs and ambushes.

About thirty minutes had gone by since the last of the grunts had disappeared into the darkness and were swallowed up by the jungle. Explosions ripped through the night, and Bear knew the LPs or ambushes had made enemy contact. The third platoon ambush patrol fought their way back to the perimeter. The camp watched helplessly from the perimeter and did not fire for fear of hitting their own men. The night lit up with green and red tracers flying in all directions. Explosions flashed in the black jungle. The 4.2 mortar team of the 5th Mechanized Infantry fired illumination rounds to light up the area so the defenders could see, and the men outside could see to retreat to safety inside the perimeter. The word passed from one to another – don't shoot, hold your fire, wait for our men to get home. The battle came closer to the perimeter as the tracers were getting closer in the dark between illumination rounds

Out of the night someone yelled, "Hold your fire! We're coming in!" Then figures appeared out of the jungle, helping each other toward the perimeter. Bear knew it was bad because he could see some of the figures being carried and dragged. Bear readied his M - 60 because he knew the VC would be right on their butt. "Damn," He thought to himself, "hope we're ready for this mess."

The figures reached the concertina wire, some were confused, trying to find their way through the wire. It seemed like a million VC came tearing out of the jungle toward the confused mob in the wire. Bear wasn't in line with the men, so he started firing his M - 60 machine gun into the VC. The first hundred round belt did not take long. The VC retreated into the jungle.

The third platoon ambush squad finally made it inside the wire, but none to soon, for another wave of VC appeared out of the jungle. Several claymores were detonated and the VC wave retreated. The first platoon's ambush area lit up as a fire fight started. The second platoon's ambush area lit up with fire power. All sides were under attack. The ambush and LPs moved back into the perimeter. The illumination rounds kept the area lit up off and on during the battle.

"Charlie" launched another attack on the perimeter. Bear fired into the figures approaching the wire. The VC seemed to be drugged because they kept coming. Bear kept firing. His M - 60 barrel heated up and glowed. Bear quickly used the asbestos glove and changed the barrel. He fired and fired. They kept coming.

Incoming mortar rounds exploded all over the base camp. A bandoleer torpedo went off under the wire to Bear's left and created a gaping hole in the wire.

The VC regrouped on Bear's side of the perimeter while the rest of the perimeter was still being rushed by the enemy. Bear quickly counted his ammo: about 500 rounds left. Five belts between Bear and who knew what.

The VC launched their attack toward the gaping hole in the wire. Bear unloaded on the first bunch. They all went down. Another wave came towards the wire. The whole platoon frantically fired. The VC got closer and closer, wave after wave. The incoming mortar rounds kept coming inside the perimeter. Bear lost count of his M - 60 rounds.

He just kept firing. The VC kept coming.

"Gooks in the wire!!" rang out in the night's battle. It meant there were VC inside the perimeter now. The artillery howitzers fired their beehive rounds. It was time for the "grunts" to keep their heads down and protect their butts. As the howitzers reloaded, Bear threw his three grenades at the gooks coming through the hole in the wire.

The howitzers fired again. Bear hugged the ground behind his sand bagged position. He took a quick count of his ammo. One half a belt, about 50 rounds left. "Lord, help me!" He yelled. Here he was along way from home with only 50 rounds of M - 60 ammo, two clips for his .45 pistol and a bayonet between him and death.

After a long silence all around the perimeter, the gooks launched a last huge effort to completely overrun the fire base. Bear fired until he ran out of ammo. He knew he couldn't be resupplied because nobody wanted to take a chance of being mistaken for a gook in the wire. He emptied one clip from his .45 pistol and then most of the other clip. Hell, he couldn't hit anything with a .45 pistol if his life depended on it - and it did. The howitzers fired point blank again. The mortar teams fired on their own perimeter. The soldiers beat the attack back into the jungle. Through the night air could be heard the calls for a medic.

"Medic! Medic! Medic!" There were groans and moans everywhere.

What time is it? Bear knew it had to be near dawn. Eleven o'clock! Twenty three hundred hours. Damn! Bear couldn't believe it. This is going to be one long, hard night.

"Bear," He heard a whisper. "Bear where are you?" For a moment he froze with fear. Then he realized the gooks didn't know his nickname.

"Yeah, over here," Bear whispered back in the dark. A figured crawled towards Bear.

It was his squad leader.

"Sarge," Bear whispered. "am I glad to see you!!"

"Bear we may still have gooks inside the wire," he whispered. "Do you need anything?"

"I need M - 60 ammo, Sarge," Bear replied.

"Here is a grenade. I'll have to go back for M - 60 rounds," Sarge whispered. "I have M - 16 ammo with me, but no M - 60 or .45 rounds."

"Thanks, Sarge, I'll be waiting." Sarge crawled off to the next position. Sarge, for some reason, never came back with Bear's ammo. There he stayed the rest of the night with about two rounds left in his .45, a grenade, and a bayonet. And it was still a long, long, night ahead.

Maybe the longest of his young life.

For some unknown reason the VC did not attack in force again. A few VC probed the perimeter with shots off and on for the rest of the night.

Just after daybreak, three dustoff evacuation choppers arrived to take the dead and wounded to Tay Ninh. The troopers helped police up the dead bodies and help the wounded to the choppers. The gooks must have carried off most of their dead during the night, or was it a horrible dream? It was ghostly to know so many were killed, only to find so few bodies.

Before the unit could finish their C - ration breakfast, the word came down for them to prepare to move out toward Tay Ninh. D Troop was to escort the artillery units to Tay Ninh.

What a waste, Bear thought to himself. We fought and some of us died for this hole in the jungle, and now we are pulling up stakes and hauling ass. But it is not a soldier's place to question the reasons. He must obey orders to the best of his ability and try to survive in the process. War sometimes is a political chess game and the soldiers are the expendable pawns. His thoughts were interrupted by the command, "Let's move out!"

The 5th Mechanized Unit that had been left at the Soui Da bridge was hit hard, also. There were three blown up APC's scattered around the bridge when the convoy arrived. Bear's gun jeep was the last vehicle in the long convoy to Tay Ninh. The twenty or so miles took all day long and they arrived at Tay Ninh about dusk. The convoy had many stops and break downs. And there was one small ambush along the way. It was a long, hard three days, like many more to come. Like a match flame blown out by the wind, Fire Base Burke was no more than a bad memory.

PREK KLOK AMBUSH

The road had already been swept and cleared earlier in the day from Prek Klok to Tay Ninh by way of Nui Ba Den (the Black Virgin Mountain as it was called). The platoon of gun jeeps were to lead a truck convoy back to Tay Ninh from Prek Klok. As the convoy moved out the gun jeeps interspersed themselves among the trucks. The narrow dirt road was grown up with jungle right up to the edge of the road. As Bear's jeep left the clearing from the fire base called the "Old French Fort", the convoy was ambushed by the Viet Cong. The last truck in the convoy, a deuce and a half carrying a very large electric generator was hit with a RPG and was on fire. Bear moved his gun jeep up behind the disabled truck as enemy rounds bounced off his gun jeep. The convoy ahead of the disabled truck was ordered to keep going. All the gun jeeps around the disabled truck dismounted and continued the fire fight on the ground with the VC.

Penguin tried to get the driver out of the burning truck. He succeeded in getting the shotgun rider out and carried him to

Bear's, jeep. Sarge called for a medivac chopper to get the wounded man to the hospital. Sarge and Bear loaded the wounded man on their jeep as bullets bounced all around them including hitting the jeep several times. The road was very narrow and Bear had a heck of a time getting turned around while Sarge administered first aid to the wounded soldier.

With bullets bouncing off the jeep Bear squeezed by the next vehicle as one of his jeep's tires was blown out by bullets. He headed the short distance to the fire base with a flat tire to meet the chopper. Bear arrived about the same time a chopper arrived. The chopper happened to be close by and heard the radio transmission for help. The wounded soldier was loaded on the chopper, and Bear headed his crippled jeep back to the fire fight which was still raging.

When they got back to the heavily burning truck, Penguin was sitting down on the ground with a far away look on his face. Sarge left to join in the fire fight.

Penguin looked up and Bear saw in his hand a billfold and a set of dogtags. Bear asked Penguin what was wrong. Penguin kept staring straight ahead and said.

"Bear, it was the most awful thing I've ever seen. I felt so helpless."

Bear knew Penguin needed to cry but he was in such shock that no tears could flow yet.

Bear said, "So Penguin tell me what happened - let it all out." After a short silence Penguin sobbed, "I went back to get the driver out of the truck, but during the explosion the generator had slid forward and pinned him to the steering wheel. I tried to pull him free, but I couldn't. The truck started burning more and more. The driver looked into my eyes with such a defeated look. He couldn't speak. He could just barely breathe. With his free right hand he jerked his dogtags off and handed them to me. He then handed me the billfold from his shirt pocket. I held his hand as long as I could. But when he started to burn and moan, I ... I!! His head dropped to his knees.

"Go on," Bear said.

31

Penguin began to cry. Bear got down on his knees and held Penguin's head to his chest.

"I thought I was going to burn up with him. He held my hand so tight and I couldn't get away. I should have stayed to the end. I should have..."

Bear broke in and said, "You did all you could, it was not your fault."

"But Bear, I can still see his eyes. Oh! My God help me." Penguin cried.

Bear patted Penguin on the back as Penguin clung to him.

"It will pass in time, Penguin - just let it all out." Bear said.

After awhile, Bear took the billfold from Penguin's hand and opened it up to an unmailed letter. It must have been addressed to his parents since it had a Mr. & Mrs. address.

Bear put it on the mail chopper later that week. As Bear handed the letter to the mail courier he notice written on the back..."To be mailed in the case of my death."

That day had come and gone.

GRANDMA'S HEAVEN

In Nam, when a unit was on stand down, they could relax a little and drink a little beer. Late in the night in base camp, after a few beers, inhibitions would be let down and the soldiers would drop their macho facade and talk about things that really mattered to all of them. They talked about home, family, life and death. Living every day, all day long so close to death, made them all contemplate what happened after death.

Bill, a Bible - belt - Baptist, often told stories of what his Grandma told him about heaven when he was a youngster. The stories were the link to the reality of death but the hope for a life after death.

Bill would start his stories by saying, "My Grandma used to tell me about heaven, especially when I was scared during a storm and such." Grandma would say, "Heaven is warm and gentle like a new spring day, warmed by a bold red sun. A gentle breeze lazily blows to cool the brow. Everyone in heaven has their hunger fulfilled and their thirst quenched. Everyone is loved and feels loved like a Grandma hugs her grandchild.

Time is spent down at the fishing hole, - fishing and napping. There are no clocks to pressure you. Everyone loves everyone. Everyone worships the Lord all day long. No bills to pay, no work to do, no things to accumulate, no house to clean, and even no beds to make. Everyone feels good all the time because there is no pain, no illness, no wars, and no evil. Our Father loves us more than we would ever know. Jesus tells endless stories.

And we play and romp in the goodness around us. Yes, Bill never be afraid of dying because in dying we live forever in heaven. I can't wait to get to heaven."

Bear would sleep soundly after those stories. It might have been the beer, but Bear preferred to think of it as his dreams of heaven.

The mission that March day was to be an easy sweep of a village to search for suspected hidden weapons. The third platoon was choppered out and let out near the village in some rice paddies. The rice paddies were dry, thank the Lord, but a soldier still had to be careful of bobby traps, especially on the dikes.

The platoon approached the village without any problems. The villagers did not seem to mind that they were there. Bear thought to himself that this was going to be an easy day. We could be back to base camp by dinner time. Bear and Bill had their M – 60 machine gun set up outside the village, pulling security just in case the VC showed up uninvited. The third squad was set up in pairs around the village on security guard while the first and second squads searched the village.

There weren't very many people in the village. That was unusual. Bear wondered, where they were. Bill and Bear talked about home and things like that while they watched and waited. "Charlie" was the master of surprises, and they were good at "hit and run" tactics.

The first sound of war Bear heard was a dozen "RPGs" (Rocket Propelled Grenades) going off at the same time. The villagers disappeared in no time flat. Bill and Bear fired into the jungle, hoping to keep "Charlie" at bay. They shot the hell out of the trees and bushes, but they never saw a VC. Explosions were hitting all around them and they hadn't seen a gook yet. Bear's position had been spotted and the VC were zeroing in on it.

Bear decided to move to a more secure area, closer to the tree line and closer to the rest of the platoon. Bear went first, zig - zagging toward the tree line. Bill followed as soon as Bear set up a defensive position. By this time, the Cobra gunships had arrived and were pouring rockets and machine gun fire all around the village. As soon as the gunships emptied their arsenal, the platoon leader ordered the platoon to move into the jungle to engage "Charlie". Bear really thought the platoon leader was more interested in getting a body count before the VC could carry off their dead.

The platoon moved into the jungle firing as they went. Bill was to Bear's right and behind him a little distance. An explosion from behind Bear knocked him to the ground.

Bear hugged the ground and waited. After a few minutes that seemed like an eternity, Bear heard a loud moan from behind him.

Bear crawled toward the sound of pain. Bear realized it was where he had seen Bill last. Bear crawled faster and reached Bill. Bill was hurt bad. He had tripped a "Bouncing Betty" mine, and it had blown up about waist high. A "Bouncing Betty" was a mine that was propelled up before it exploded. It was a deadly mine. Bear tried to keep Bill calm as he surveyed the wounds. Bear called for a "Medic" several times and finally Doc showed up. Doc and Bear worked on Bill to patch him up and stop the bleeding.

Bill had more holes in him than Bear could count. "Hang in there, Bill," Bear said.

"It's gonna be okay. Doc will take care of you, just remain calm."

"Bear," Bill said, "It's real bad, ain't it?"

"No it's gonna be all right. Just hang in there."

Doc had to go elsewhere to help the other wounded, but he told Bear to keep pressure on the chest and stomach bandages. Bear couldn't believe this was happening. Hell, no one had even seen a gook. What a way to fight a war. The firing had all but stopped. Then it was over. How do you battle an unseen enemy? It was frustrating to say the least.

The platoon waited for the "slick" (slicks being empty choppers used for transporting) choppers to come in to pick up the wounded. Bill broke Bear's train of thought. He said, "Bear, tell me again about Grandma's heaven. I'm scared."

Bear almost choked. "Bill, you're going to be okay."

"Please Bear," Bill gasped, "tell me about heaven." With this plea, Bear couldn't help but tell Bill what he wanted to hear. Bear started rambling about Bill's Grandma's heaven. It seemed to quiet Bill, so Bear kept talking to him.

The slicks came in and Bear helped load Bill on the chopper. Bear rode with him and kept pressure on his wounds. The ride was noisy because there were no doors on the chopper. They were open to the wind and motor noise. As Bear's chopper lifted off the ground, Bear could see more "slicks" coming in to pick up the rest of the troops and fly them back to base camp. Bear felt numb from the day's experience, but a gentle tug on his sleeve brought him back to reality. Bill motioned with his eyes for him to come closer so Bear could hear him. Bear put his ear to Bill's mouth.

"Bear, tell me about heaven. I think I may be going there soon." Bill spoke into Bear's ear. Bear looked into Bill's pleading eyes. There was a twinkle in Bill's eyes - a happiness, an inner peace. Bear put his mouth to Bill's ear and told him what he wanted to hear.

"Heaven is like a warm, spring day, warmed by the sun. Birds sing. The fishing hole is teeming with fish. There is no pain and no wars. Love fills the air and your Grandma is there waiting with open, loving arms," Bear said. On and on Bear rambled.

As the chopper approached Cu Chi base camp, Bear felt Bill sigh. Bear looked at Bill's face. Bill had a satisfied smile on his face. Bill had gone to see his Grandma, and Bear cried. God, Bear thought, please help me find Bill's kind of faith someday.

THE LATERITE GRAVEL PIT

Each platoon rotated daytime assignments everyday. At night each platoon had every third night off unless something came up. At night, one platoon had ambush patrols, one platoon had perimeter guard duty, and one platoon stayed in their unit hooches unless needed. In the day time, one platoon had convoy guard duty from around the Trang Bang area back to Tay Ninh, one platoon guarded the engineer trucks hauling gravel to and from their destination, and one platoon had security duty at the laterite gravel pits where the heavy equipment dug up and loaded the gravel into trucks.

May 15, 1968, started at 0200 with the first mortar attack. Bear had written letters and visited until midnight, and had just gotten to sleep when that first barrage of mortars and rockets hit Tay Ninh base camp. Bear rolled off his cot onto the floor and covered his head until the short attack was over. The U.S. artillery and mortars returned fire for several more minutes.

After the firing stopped, Bear looked outside to make sure the area had not been hit. The area was okay so Bear crawled back in his cot to sleep. At 0400 mortars and rockets awakened Bear again, although they were not as close this time. Bear stayed in his cot and listened to the artillery battery return fire. The VC fired a few rounds and then moved to another location to fire again. It was what was called harassing fire. D troop's base camp area was located by a tall empty water tower and Bear always figured the VC used it as an aiming stake to adjust fire into the main base camp.

At 0530, the platoon was awakened for their day's work. Bear had just put his feet on the floor about 0600 and was trying to get awake when incoming rounds hit again. This time it was close enough so that Bear headed for the bunker. As Bear left the "hooch" for the bunker, He noticed that the motor pool had been hit and a vehicle was on fire.

This was the first time in a long time that the VC had bombarded the area in the day time. As it turned out the VC continued bombarding the base camp off and on all day long. At breakfast, Bear learned that the Special Forces communications unit on top of the Black Virgin (Nui Ba Den) Mountain Northeast of Tay Ninh had been under siege all night long. During the night the second platoon had been airlifted onto the mountain to help fortify the position. Many of the Special Forces were killed, but the second platoon and the Special Forces finally beat off the attack about dawn.

The third platoon was responsible for security at the laterite gravel pit this fine (ha-ha) day. Tay Ninh's North side perimeter was hit by a ground attack in the night. An RPG {rocket propelled grenade} had killed two U.S. soldiers. A few gooks had been killed. Bear was the scout squad leader's gun jeep driver this day. The first job was to clear the road to the gravel pit and then secure the area around the pit before the engineers arrived. About dusk last night, chopper gunships had called in that they had killed about ten VC at the pit. When the platoon got to the gravel pit, they met an ARVN unit leaving the area. The scout squad leader visited with their commander and found out the ARVNs had secured the area. The ARVNs had found many blood trails but no

VC bodies. Typically, the VC had carried the bodies away like thieves in the night.

The platoon set up a perimeter around the pit with their gun jeeps and trucks. By noon, the area was swamped with Vietnamese prostitutes and children selling cokes.

The platoon should have known something was up since there were four times more Vietnamese around the pit than usual. The VC were smart, and they knew how to get the American's attention off their business, The whores practically gave their wares away— another reason the platoon should have been wary. Bear's jeep was parked facing the Vam Co Dong River. Bear could hear mortars and rockets firing and exploding in the distance. As was learned later, Tay Ninh was fired on every hour all day long with about six rounds per hour. The American artillery fired return fire off and on all day. The platoon medic was called back to Tay Ninh, and he took Bear's gun jeep with most of the extra ammo. Bear and his crew took up position on the river bank facing the river. The Vietnamese kept bothering the soldiers and for good reason. They were to keep the soldiers busy while the VC set up position across the river to ambush the ARVN river patrol boat that patrolled up and down the river everyday.

In a moment of time, most of the civilians left. They vanished from sight. At that time, the gunner and squad leader were lying down by the river. Bear was throwing his bayonet at a tree killing time. The ARVN river patrol boat came down the river. The platoon waved as the boat passed by headed downstream. As the boat rounded a bend in the river almost out of sight, the VC sprang the ambush from across the river. The platoon grabbed their rifles and took up position along the river bank to return fire. There was a volley of bullets flying from across the river. Mac was next to Bear with his M - 60 machine gun. The few civilians that were still there started yelling "No VC" and running out of the area.. The engineers quickly found a hiding place and took up fighting positions.

Deafened by the return fire, Bear failed to notice the thud of 60 MM mortars headed his way. Being trained as a 81MM mortar man, Bear was the first to notice the short rounds hitting the river water as "Charlie" walked the mortar rounds towards the platoon. Most of the VC small arms fire had stopped, but rifle grenades and mortar rounds and probably even some captured M - 79 rounds took the place of the small arms fire.

The squad leader ordered the squad to fire and maneuver back up the river bank out of sight and possibly out of range. This kind of fight was so irritating because the squad had not yet spotted a single VC soldier, but the squad was catching hell. Bear moved back about 30 meters and set up to cover fire while Mac and the other two soldiers moved back. Fire and maneuver, but Bear called it retreat. The platoon shot the hell out of the woodline across the river. The fight between the VC and the patrol boat could be heard in the distance. It sounded as if the patrol boat was trying to escape down river.

Mac and his bunch moved back to Bear's position, and as Bear got up to move back, he tripped and fell down. As Bear rolled back to his feet, he could see the trees starting to explode. Oh, hell, he thought — can we out run them?

Bear and Mac set up and signalled the others to move back. A "newbee" (green recruit) froze and wouldn't move when the others moved out. The mortar and grenade rounds exploded all around him. The squad leader picked up a tree limb and threw it at the "newbee". The limb hit the "newbee" in the back and like a shot, he ran back towards Bear. As he left his forward position, it exploded into a million pieces.

All the trees started exploding in front of the squad. The squad panicked and ran toward the gravel pit. Several rounds hit the taller trees around Bear. Bear's ears were deafened by the explosions. The concussions lifted Bear up and twisted him in mid air and tossed him to the hard ground about ten feet away. Bear landed on his right side with his right arm and M - 16 rifle under him.

Bear couldn't hear a thing but the ringing in his ears. Bear saw yellow and white spots in front of his eyes, and he felt sick to his stomach.

The squad leader grabbed Bear and helped him to his feet. The squad leader's lips were moving but Bear couldn't hear a thing. He pointed at Bear's right arm as they ran to safety. Bear glanced down to see blood spurting down his right lower arm. Every time Bear's heart beat, and his heart was beating very, very fast, blood spurted down his arm. Bear's first thought was that his arm was blown apart. Somehow, Bear's poncho had fallen out from his web belt where it had been tied, and tripped him again and again until he got untangled. His whole right side felt bruised and started to ache, and he still could not hear a thing.

Cobra gunships arrived and the mortar barrage stopped. The VC were retreating now. Bear got to a jeep and the squad leader put a compress bandage on his elbow. The bleeding stopped and Bear was sure relieved. They climbed in the jeep and the squad leader took him back to Tay Ninh base camp at about 100 m.p.h.. Bear thought Sarge was going to wreck them a few times but they made it.

As they were headed in, Bear happened to look at his M - 16 rifle which he still had clutched in his right hand by the top carrying handle. The pistol grip, part of the butt, and part of the forward grip were blown off the rifle. Bear thought "his rifle got torn up worse than he did." He started laughing hysterically. Sarge hollered at Bear and asked him what the hell was so funny. Bear could barely hear him. The ringing was lower but Sarge's voice sounded as if he were talking in a barrel. Bear hollered back, "I'm alive, but my rifle isn't so good."

Bear was delivered to the camp hospital, and Sarge went back to the gravel pit. The male nurse put Bear on a table and started cleaning the wound. His wounded arm was still numb. He had not yet felt any extreme pain, just numbness, but he knew he had been wounded because of all the blood.

All of a sudden, the latrine behind the hospital exploded as the incoming rocket siren blasted. The medics helped all of the wounded into the bunker next to the hospital. As the rocket attack raged outside the bunker, the doctor deadened the area around Bear's elbow and dug around in the wound to find the shrapnel. He could feel the pulling and pushing, but he couldn't feel any pain. The doctor checked him for a concussion and found he had a slight concussion. The doctor checked Bear's ears but luckily nothing was ruptured. Bear watched the doctor probe on him for about twenty minutes. The doctor couldn't get the shrapnel. It was imbedded in the bone. The doctor told Bear he didn't want to take a chance of severing any nerve endings, so he quit.

The doctor gave Bear a tetanus shot and bandaged him up. The doctor told him to change the bandage every few hours to keep down the infection and to check each bandage to see if the shrapnel might work itself out. He was told to come back in three days so he could check it and put stitches in the wound at that time. This was to give the shrapnel a chance to come out and to make sure there was not going to be any infection. The doctor gave him some Darvon for pain. Bear didn't know until many years later that darvon was addictive. Hell, in Nam the soldiers popped them like candy for aches and pains and for the proverbial hangover.

About the time the group started out of the bunker, another rocket barrage hit the base camp, so they just waited out the attack in the bunker. By the time Bear got back to his unit area, he had a terrific headache and his elbow started to hurt. His right side was real sore. So he popped a few Darvon and got a little high.

The third platoon came in about the time Bear got to the hootch. The choppers and the third platoon didn't even find VC or a VC body. Damn gooks anyway. TOP (Troop Sergeant Major) told Bear he would get a Purple Heart, but he was not going to loaf around. A few days later, Bear got stitches put in his wound. The shrapnel stayed in his arm, and it is still in his elbow to this day. He sets off the alarm in the airports everytime.

The troop spent most of that day and night in the bunkers as the VC rocketed them every hour, and the troop was on red alert all night to be ready to reinforce the perimeter if an attack occurred. The platoon mortar squad fired all night. They were set up in the motor pool. Bear's last thought that day was I hope I never come that close to death again.

"CHEROKEE" - THE BATTLE OF BEN MUONG

February through May, 1968, D Troop pulled gravel pit security and convoy duty on Route # 1 between Cu Chi and Tay Ninh, Viet Nam. The convoy moved much needed food, supplies, and ammo to Tay Ninh before the rainy season came. The gravel pit provided gravel to build and upgrade roads in the Tay Ninh area. As the time got closer to May, the fighting became intense along the highway. By the middle of May, the action in the area was heavy. At night the rockets and ground attacks occurred everywhere at once and at any time of night or day. "Charlie" was really very active, and it made life a little more hell.

D Troop was busy day and night. At night the three platoons rotated among ambush, perimeter guard, and staying at the hooch area as ready standby. Of course, the ready - standby got a little sleep, so every three nights, one platoon could get some rest until the rockets and mortars started hitting the area.

51

During the daytime, each platoon rotated among convoy duty, gravel pit security, and ready standby at the unit area to offer assistance in case the two platoons made contact and needed backup. Snipers and ambush were the big problems along the highway during the day. Both Route #1 and the gravel pit were in no fire zones, which meant the U.S. soldiers could not shoot unless they were shot at first.

Duty at the gravel pit consisted of sweeping the area and setting up security so that the engineers could dig up the gravel to be hauled to other areas, mainly to build roads. The gravel pit was several miles from Tay Ninh base camp, along the Vam Co Dong River. Foot patrols were sent out at different times of the day to check out the area and make sure the area wasn't surprised or overrun by "Charlie". When the gravel trucks were loaded, part of the unit would escort them to their destination and back. It was a tedious, boring job with most days going by with only a sniper or two harassing the troops.

The convoy duty started from the front gate at Tay Ninh base camp. D Troop had no mine sweepers. The lead gun jeeps were the mine sweepers. A sharp eye by the standing gunner would detect any disturbance of the ground ahead of the jeep. The scout jeeps were staggered fifty meters apart with one jeep in the middle of the road, one on the right side of the road, and one on the left side of the road. The platoon would sweep the road to Go Dau Ha, Trang Bang, or at times to Cu Chi. When the road was swept and secured, the platoon would pick up the truck convoy from another unit and escort the convoy back to Tay Ninh. The trucks were loaded with food, drinks, fuel, ammo, and other supplies. The platoon would lead the way with one scout gun jeep and the other gun jeeps dispersed among the trucks. The convoy would try to keep fifty meters between vehicles in case of an ambush. That way "Charlie" couldn't stack up a bunch of vehicles at one place.

Normally, when a sniper would fire at the convoy, the convoy would keep moving and pray no damage was done. The nearest gun jeep would check out the sniper area. In most cases, "Charlie" had beat it out of the area. Harassment was the name of that game. Every once in a while, "Charlie" would blow a bridge during the day or fire mortar rounds at the highway.

May 29th started too early, as usual at 0530. Bear was the M - 60 machine gunner on the first scout gun jeep.

Bear's usual jeep commander went on sick call with a bad case of the hemorrhoids. Bear kidded him that morning that the Army didn't give Purple Hearts for hemorrhoids, no matter how painful. By his half - hearted chuckle, Bear could tell he was in pain. Bear was sure that the occasional dysentery, of which Sarge had a bad case, didn't help matters much either.

The third platoon pulled out of the front gate about 0630. In their briefing, they had been told that intelligence had information that there was about 1,000 VC regulars across the Vam Co Dong River, Southeast of Highway #1 somewhere in the Go Dau Hau area, probably base camped in Cambodia. The platoon proceeded to Tay Ninh village with no trouble. Just outside the village there was an ARVN compound. It was a small outpost with probably fifty ARVNS and their families. As Bear's jeep turned the corner to head past the compound, the road was blocked with carts and other debris. The scouts checked it out and moved the stuff off the road.

The ARVN compound had been overrun by the VC and the VC had massacred the whole compound, including women and children. Bodies, blood, and destruction were everywhere. God, it made Bear sick to his stomach. The policeman in charge gave Bear the scoop. It seemed someone inside the compound had unlocked the gate and let the VC in before anyone knew what hit them. Bear called back to the platoon leader at the rear of the column and relayed the information. The scouts proceeded down the highway, cautiously, of course. Just before they got to the rubber plantation area that lined part of the highway, Bear's jeep came upon a large road block. They found two grenade booby traps and blew them up along with the road block. The other scouts helped clear the debris and shovel dirt back in the holes. The road was rough enough as it was. Just ask Bear's squad leader.

Bear's jeep approached one very small village, a shot came from the rubber plantation. The bullet was so close to Bear's head that he could feel the heat as it went by his head. Bear almost filled his drawers.

Mac, the driver, made an immediate left, and they started through the rubber trees ninety - to - nothing. He almost threw Bear off the jeep when he started out but Bear managed to hold on.

Sarge turned around and looked up at Bear and asked, "Are you okay, Bear? Keep your eyes open,"

Bear replied, "Okay, Sarge," while trying to act cool, as if he had everything under control.

They bounced around, swerving in and out around the rubber trees. Bear fired a few bursts here and there, trying to flush out the sniper. Nothing. The VC seemed to have disappeared into thin air.

"Blue Tiger 32, this is 36, over," came the call from the platoon leader.

"This is Blue Tiger 32, over," answered Sarge.

"32 what is going on up there? We've been stopped a long time, and we heard explosions and gunfire. You know we have to rendezvous with the convoy sometime today."

"Roger, 36. We are returning to the road. We had a sniper, and blew some booby traps. We'll be moving soon."

Bear's jeep made it back to the road and started toward Go Dau Hau. They were flagged down by a woman who seemed very upset. She said in broken English that the sniper had been shooting and harassing them all night and day. Sarge told her that they didn't find him. Needless to say, she wasn't relieved.

The road was clear until they got to the edge of Go Dau Hau. A mortar round hit about thirty meters from the jeep and blew up a hooch.

"Wow! That was close," Sarge hollered. "31 and 33, this is 32. Move up in a hurry and let's try to find this mortar crew that just tried to blow us to hell!"

Off all the scout jeeps went around the outside edge of the village trying to find the mortar crew. They found nothing. There was no telling where the VC mortar crew was located.

The scout jeeps got back into position and proceeded through the village and on toward Trang Bang. Strange, Bear thought, there was no traffic on the road and the village was sure quiet. There was not much activity around anywhere. That was a clue that something was going to happen very soon. D Troop met the convoy at Trang Bang and headed back toward Tay Ninh without any problems.

Bear's jeep came to Tay Ninh village and started across the river bridge when he heard a M - 16 round fired.

"32, come back here!" the radio blurted. Mac turned the jeep around and headed back toward Tay Ninh village.

"What the hell is going on?" Bear's Sergeant asked as his jeep pulled up to the other jeeps.

"Phil shot a boy in the leg, Sarge," 31 said. Phil was drunk. He had sat down in the jeep and had his M - 16 on his lap. He was the machine gunner, but he couldn't even stand up. The Vietnamese boy was being attended to by some people, but man, were they all mad. Bear couldn't blame them. It seemed the boy had shot Phil with a AK - 101 which was a pea shooter of sorts made out of bamboo. A pebble or pea was popped through the bamboo with a plunger. Phil was drunk, and he shot before he thought. He had been drinking a lot since he had gotten a "Dear John" letter from his fiancee.

"Damn it, Phil! What am I going to do with you? You trying to ruin your life?" Sarge barked.

"I don't care," Phil said. "The kid hit me first."

Sarge, shaking his head, went over to the group and talked with them for a while. He returned and asked Phil, "How much money do you have on you?"

"About fifty bucks in MPC (Military Payment Certificates). Why?"

"Let me have it. I think we can buy out of this."

"But Sarge."

"Damn it, Phil the lieutenant will be up here in a while and he'll hang your ass."

Phil gave him the money. The GIs weren't suppose to let the gooks have MPC, but it was common especially if a soldier didn't have any piasters, (Vietnamese money). Sarge went over and gave the boy the money and apologized. The scouts hauled out of there just in time, too.

"32, this is 36, what is the hold up? Over."

"We are on our way, 36, just a little traffic jam."

The platoon and convoy made it to Tay Ninh base camp without any further problems. The platoon ate supper and assembled in their hooches with all their gear for their night assignment. The third platoon had ambush duty tonight. The platoon would exit the gate and thus began another long night. Bear would have gate guard duty at the gate the platoon would go out. The gate guards locked the gate after the platoon left at dusk. Since Phil was still drunk, he would be left with Bear at the gate. Bear would be up most of the night. The platoon sergeant sure didn't want Phil on the ambush. The gate guard's duty consisted of monitoring the radio in case the platoon made contact. A call would be made every hour on the hour for a radio check. The troop mortar crew was set up in the troop motor pool area for fire support.

The platoon all cleaned their weapons and laid down to rest a while before the night shift began. Bear had a hard time getting Phil awake, but Phil finally got around. The platoon was hauled to the front gate in a deuce and a half (2 1/2 ton truck).

Bear told Phil to go ahead and sleep, and he would take the first watch. Bear listened to his transistor radio to Armed Forces radio until about 0130. It was a quiet night, Bear woke Phil up and after Phil seemed to be okay. Bear dozed off. A few minutes later Phil woke Bear up.

"Bear, wake up! I can't stay awake no more."

"What time is it?"

"0200.

"Damn, Phil. You're going to have to quit drinking. I'm getting tired of carrying your load." Bear was always grumpy when he first woke up, especially when he had no rest for a few days and nights.

"Sorry, Bear," Phil said, and immediately fell asleep.

It was along time until 0630, but the time went by fast because the platoon ambush was receiving probing sniper fire. That meant that "Charlie" wasn't sure where the ambush was located so they were shooting in hopes of drawing fire.

Bear listened to the squads talking to one another. When the platoon came in at 0630, Bear learned that a new E-5 squad leader, fresh out of headquarters troop, had screwed up again. The ambush was to be a triangle shaped position. He had gotten lost in the dark and had never linked up his squad with the sides of the triangle. His squad was to be the base of the triangle. Instead, there was a gap on each side where the sides didn't connect to the base. The worst part was that their positions were pointed toward the other positions, and they had their back to the enemy. Bear kept hoping the E-5 wouldn't get someone killed with his blunders.

The day was May 30, 1968, the traditional Memorial Day holiday. D Troop would have no holiday. The third platoon ate breakfast and cleaned up and then laid down to rest. It was their day to be ready standby. The first platoon went to the gravel pit. The second platoon had convoy duty. The troop medic, Doc, went with the second platoon since their medic was on R & R. Cherokee was Doc's best friend and a good friend of Bear. Doc and Cherokee had joined the Army and had gone through basic training together.

"Cherokee", as he told it, was a full blood Cherokee Indian from the Southern part of Pennsylvania along the West Virginia state line. His real name was John Sinnock. He was about 5_10" and 190 pounds with dark hair and piercing dark brown eyes. He was a good natured man with a good since of humor. "Cherokee" was a good soldier.

About 1000 hours, the call came that the second platoon had been ambushed at Bien Muong and were pinned down. The third platoon immediately got ready to go help on a moment's notice. From the radio transmissions, it was learned that five men had been dusted off (medically evacuated), three walking and two carried (probably dead).

Doc told Bear what happened at a later time. The day was like all others on the convoy duty. Snipers, blocked roads, and booby traps were found as usual. As the lead gun jeep came close to Bien Moung, they received sniper fire and saw enemy movement on the North side of the road. The area was on a slight incline with dirt berm surrounding the area. Most villages had dirt berms surrounding them for protection and from flooding during the rainy season. The gun jeep called for backup and a 106 anti-tank jeep moved up to help. The two jeeps came on line and headed North about fifty meters to a church and graveyard area, where they stopped.

At that moment, they were unknowingly in the middle of a whole company of VC dug-in in their spider holes and bunkers. The church was their headquarters.

"Cherokee" was hit bad. Cherokee was dragged over the berm to safety. The rest of the platoon had gotten there by now and they set up positions on the berm, firing at the VC. Doc arrived and started patching up the wounded. "Cherokee's" chest was laid open, and he was barely alive when Doc found him. "Cherokee" died in his best friends arms that day as the battle raged on around them.

Doc was never the same after that time. He started using drugs to ease the pain. The Troop lost a good man that day. They lost part of Doc that day, too.

The XO woke Bear up at about 10 am. He wanted Bear to drive him to the battle site. Bear drove as fast as he could. When

Bear pulled up to the fighting area, the Cobra gun ships were pounding the area and the guys on the berm were shooting like crazy. The word was that the platoon was kicking the hell out of them. The XO ordered Bear to stay with the jeep as the XO ran to the berm to check out the fighting. When Bear got the word about Cherokee, he was stunned. He didn't know what to feel. Bear was numb. A touch of guilt spread over Bear. After all, the third platoon had trouble there yesterday. Why didn't they see anything? Why didn't this happen yesterday? Why didn't they see the enemy digging in? The day before, they knew it was oddly quiet. They knew there was no traffic and no civilian movement. Death was so sudden and final, and Bear didn't even have a chance to say goodbye. D troop had only one more day of convoy duty when this tragedy occurred. That in itself compounded the pain.

D troop was credited with 33 VC regular kills. The third platoon swept the area the next day after the bombers blew up the area. D Troop captured 2 VC flags. One ended up in the orderly room. The unit D Troop whipped was a top notch unit, but D

Troop kicked their butt. The third platoon blew about fifteen spider holes and bunkers. The church had been used as the command post where they found plasma, bloody bandages, and other medical supplies. The third platoon finished sweeping and destroying the area and joined the convoy going back to Tay Ninh.

June 2, 1968, a memorial service for "Cherokee" was held in troop formation. A M-16 with bayonet attached was stuck in the ground with a helmet and dog tags hanging from the rifle butt. A bugler played Taps as the troop gave "Cherokee" a salute and final send off. A tear ran down Bear's cheek. A lump formed in his throat, "So long, "Cherokee." May you rest in peace in the happy hunting grounds forever.

CHEROKEE
by Ken Williams

(Dedicated to John Sinnock, "Cherokee" who gave his life for God and Country on May 30, 1968.)

A smile on his dark face you could always see.

This "West Virginie" Hillbilly, Cherokee.

The little, black, curly mustache he wore with great pride

was the only sign of the Frenchman - his Father's side.

His Dear Mother, a fair Cherokee maiden,

Gave to him his quiet nature so laden,

With a daring but dear, friendly personality.

He was a fairly, big man — my brave friend, Cherokee.

As this Vietnam War has pulled so many fine men down,

Cherokee, one fighting - filled day lay dead on the ground.

For though only an infantry sergeant in the U.S. Cavalry,

His men always came first — and there we lost "Ole Cherokee".

His best friend — blood brother — a medic we called Doc,

Would with the help of whiskey and memories of Sinnock,

Sing us by the hours, long ballads of the U.S. 17th Cavalry,

And the brother of us all "Ole West Virginia Hillbilly Cherokee".

CHOPPER CRASH

D Troop awoke when it was still dark to go on a search and destroy mission that June morning. The scuttlebutt was that a repatriated "gook" had pinpointed a NVA unit in the Phouc Vinh area. The mission was to be a three day troop - size mission.

The troop was to be inserted at sunrise. Each of the three area checkpoints were about three clicks apart from one another. They had to march three clicks in the heavy woodlands each day. The truth was that most of the "heavy woodlands" were solid jungle.

Bear was the scout leader's RTO. The three scout squads were in the first sortie to be inserted to secure the LZ. The scouts were inserted with no problem. As soon as the rest of the troop was inserted, the three scout squads headed - up the three prong sweep and swept the jungle toward their first checkpoint, three long, hot humid clicks away.

The first day passed without incident. The troop found very little signs of the enemy.

In fact they just got dog - tired for nothing. The troop set up a perimeter for the night and sent out LPs and ambushes. Bear went out on LP (listening post) with two other grunts. It was a long hot night. Not a round or flare was fired all night. It was unbelievably quiet.

The second day started out much like the first. About noon things changed. The troop encountered many booby traps of all kinds throughout the afternoon which hampered their progress through the bush. The troop had several dust - offs with heat exhaustion that second afternoon, and the troop had never even seen one "gook".

The troops were always exhausted. They would not get much sleep the night before because of LPs, ambushes, and guard duty only resting a few hours at a time then awake for several hours. The days were spent hacking thru the jungle with machetes in 100 degree heat and 100% humidity. The rests were few and far between. The water was scarce. The food was "C" rations at best. The exercise was all a person could ever want and then some. The tension was on - going not knowing when and where a battle might happen. This went on day after day and night after night. The mosquitoes, the ants, and the leeches were everywhere and they just seemed to fall out of the bushes.

It was the toughest work imaginable. The scout squads ran into several well - traveled trails.

Each platoon spread out and checked each trail area thoroughly. Nothing turned up. The troop did not make their second checkpoint until almost dusk.

The troop was all dead tired, but they had to prepare for the long night. With all of the signs that had been found today, the leaders thought that the enemy would surely probe the troops position that night. Bear didn't know where he got the energy to keep going.

The instinct to survive kept all the troopers going.

That night there were many probes throughout the night around the perimeter, but nothing major happened. The night lasted ten years at least. Every little thing irritated Bear tremendously. The bugs, the humid heat, the dark, black night, all loomed heavy on his mind. Bear hated that feeling of being out of control. Before daylight came, Bear aged another year at least.

The third day was the toughest day. The only thing that kept the troops going was the fact that they would be picked up and flown to base camp at the end of the day.

About mid morning the scout squads found what they had been searching for all along. Bear called back to the platoon leader.

"Blue Tiger 36 this is 32 Delta, over."

"Go ahead 32 Delta, over," LT answered.

"We've come upon a bunker complex. It looks like a large unit camp, over."

"Let's check it out. I'll contact the CO, out."

The base camp was definitely a NVA base camp. It was the largest and best built Bear had ever seen. The gooks had just left. The fires were still hot and cooked food had been left behind. They found several large mess - hall size bunkers with benches and tables. Why did "Charlie" just up and leave? The troop was ordered to find the VC trail and give chase. The third platoon was left behind to blow the complex. The first and second platoons gave chase. As soon as the third platoon had blown the complex, they were to follow the other platoons.

It took the platoon two hours to blow the complex with C - 4 explosives. By the time they had finished, the other two platoons had returned. They had not found "Charlie", and the troop was directed to secure an LZ to be picked up by 1800. The troop secured an LZ within 100 meters of the former complex.

The third platoon would be the last one extracted, so they had security around the LZ.

The scout squad would be the last to leave— Bear guessed that was fair since they were the first to land. Ha! Ha!

Bear was wringing wet with sweat. The sweat burned his eyes as it ran down his forehead. Bear sat and watched the jungle and daydreamed of home.

The LZ was large enough for three choppers to land simultaneously. By the time the first two platoons had been extracted, Bear developed a lonely, sick feeling in his stomach.

Bear's heart raced as he kept having these feelings of being left behind. What if the choppers didn't come back in time? What if "Charlie" attacked right now?

Bear knew that he wouldn't get to leave until the last chopper, because he knew that his squad leader would not leave until everyone else was gone. They all waited until they heard the sortie coming before pulling in their LPs. The "birds" came in sight but there were only two choppers. Bear developed a knot in his chest and a lump in his throat.

"Damn! There won't be enough room for us all." Bear thought. The two choppers banked and came into the LZ. About the time they landed, a third chopper appeared over the tree tops. "Whew!" Bear thought. His spirits rose. But Bear still had the feeling of impending doom. Bear felt that the chopper couldn't get there fast enough. As the first two lifted off the LZ, the third chopper touched down. The scouts all scrambled aboard. Bear felt relief as they started to rise.

The explosions shattered Bear's moment of tranquillity. They had taken enemy fire.

Cries of pain and flying glass filled the air. The chopper was going down fast in a circle motion dropping like a rock. Bear gripped tighter to hang on to the death trap, afraid of falling. Then he could hold on no more. Bear was flung from the chopper like a rag doll tossed aside.

Bear hit the ground with a thud, landing on his butt. The whole event happened in a moment but it was like slow motion. Bear was numb and saw stars. His back was jammed. He hurt all over but there was no blood and no broken bones. Bear was in his own world for a minute and suffered a slight concussion. Reality came back quickly because Bear knew he had to get to the chopper to help the others before it blew up.

Bear half ran — half crawled back to the chopper. The pilots were dead. His side door gunner was dead. There was no one left on the chopper.

"Bear! Bear!" He could hardly hear his name. Someone was calling him, but Bear could see no one.

The Sgt. finally got to Bear and pulled him away from the chopper. The woodline was alive with "gooks". They had circled around and come back behind, getting to the LZ in time for the last chopper to leave. Bear couldn't find his rifle so Sarge gave him an M - 60 machine gun from the chopper. Bear saw the other two choppers circle the LZ and then disappear behind them in the trees! Bear thought surely they're coming back to help us. Bear fired several bursts from the M - 60 to keep charlie busy.

Unknown to the survivors of the crash, the rest of the third platoon had been reinserted at an LZ a short distance from them to their rear. The other two platoons were being flown back to help out and several Cobra gunships were being sent ahead for support.

In the meantime, Bear fired at the enemy he could not see. They knew the enemy was still near because they could here the AK – 47's firing. The NVA must have hit the chopper with a RPG because the front was blown out. The chopper never did catch fire.

The helicopter crew had lost three people - the two pilots and one of the door gunners.

The rest of the group was in fair shape, considering what had happened. The other door gunner had a broken arm. The squad had some cuts and abrasions, but at least they were alive.

Within fifteen minutes, the Cobra gunship arrived and the squad leader popped smoke and gave the direction of the enemy. The gunships saved the soldiers tails, as they did many times in Nam. The Cobras blasted the woodline.

By the time the rest of the platoon arrived, the NVA had quit firing and were on the run. When the rest of the troop arrived, they swept the area around the LZ. Bear popped a few Darvon to ease his jammed back pain and his headache. The troop found some blood trails but no bodies. After the Chinook crane chopper picked up the wrecked chopper and left for base camp, rear command decided to abandon the search for the time being. Just about dusk, the troop was all extracted and flown to base camp for a rest.

The enemy ghost had disappeared into the bush. And the Americans disappeared back to base camp. Just another battle; or was it a battle? Who was the winner? What was won? What was the point? Bear contemplated these questions. But like a good soldier, in the end, Bear did what he was told without question.

BITTER SWEET FOREVER

July 1, 1968, Bien Hoa, Viet Nam, started out like most other days in the country, but the day soon became embedded in Bear's memory forever. If Bear had been back home, his wife and him would have celebrated their first wedding anniversary. Today Bear would not celebrate.

At 1030 the third platoon loaded three choppers for a mission North of Bien Hoa in the bush. D Troop was working with "F" Company 51st LRRP teams as a reactionary force. The LRRPs would either make enemy contact or find something for D Troop to check-out. The troopers would jump on the choppers and fly wherever to give the LRRPs a hand.

The area where the platoon was going was a free - fire zone; which meant that anything that moved was a potential target or dead meat. The opposite of a free - fire zone was a no - fire zone. A no - fire zone meant that you couldn't shoot unless someone shot at you.

No - fire areas were found around the more populated areas. Bear referred to the no – fire zone as the "sitting duck zone." In the free fire zone, there would be no question whether you were fighting the enemy if you made contact.

The mission was to meet a "F" Company 51st LRRP (Long Range Reconnaissance Patrol) team to help blow up dud mortar rounds and dig up what was thought to be a grave or ammo hiding place by a forked trail. Sometimes the VC would bury guns and ammo for a future time when they needed them, or bury their dead bodies to retrieve later.

The day was very humid since it had rained hard every evening all week. You could cut the air with a knife, it was so thick. The LZ was a small one; only one chopper could come in at a time. The platoon had brought rappelling gear because it wasn't clear whether a chopper could land at all. They did not have to rappel into the LZ which was okay with Bear.

Bear did not like the idea hanging from a rope attached to the chopper. He was too much of a target.

The LRRP team had popped smoke and set up a secure perimeter around the LZ.

As soon as the first chopper unloaded the first squad, the first squad spread out into the perimeter and helped set up security.

Bear was with the new Lieutenant platoon leader as the RTO in the second chopper.

It was always hell breaking in a new platoon leader. Most of the LTs were all right guys, but some of them were not too wise in the field of combat. This new leader seemed to know his stuff, but he was green and hadn't been tested yet.

After the third squad had come in and dismounted with no problems, the platoon started digging the supposed grave or hiding place area. They had brought several long handled shovels for the job. The second squad helped the platoon sergeant blow three dud mortar rounds with the help of a little C-4 explosive. The VC would use the dud mortar rounds in a Booby Trap if they were left intact.

The first squad had put out listening posts down the three trails about forty meters to warn the platoon in the case of enemy movement.

As Bear's chopper came in, He noticed that there was a T-shaped trail in the middle of the LZ. When they landed, one of the LRRPs showed Bear some bicycle tracks on the trails. It looked as if some gooks had been on this trail very recently. Bicycles in the jungle? Unbelievable! That was the way they moved guns and ammo and equipment.

After digging for over an hour and moving six feet of earth, it was decided that whatever had been there, was gone now.

"Bear, call base camp and tell them to send the choppers for us," said the LT.

"Roger, dodger, LT." Bear smiled when he said this, but the LT didn't return the smile. The LT did not have a sense of humor.

"White Horse 26, this is Blue Tiger 36 Delta, do you read me, over" Bear said into the mike.

"Roger, Blue Tiger 36 Delta, this is White Horse 26, What do you need, Over."

"White Horse 26, we are ready to be picked up at the same LZ where we dismounted.

Let us know when you are in the area and we'll pop smoke, over."

"Roger, Blue Tiger 36 Delta. We will be on our way in about thirty minutes, over."

"Roger that White Horse 26, out."

Bear passed along the info. It appeared that this would be a short day. The choppers would be there in less than an hour. The LRRPs would be coming in with the platoon today. It was their time to come out of the bush for a few days stand- down, which meant a little rest for them. Good thing, too. They stunk pretty bad. Man it was really getting hot and muggy, and the bugs were driving Bear crazy. It seemed that every time he opened his mouth to breathe, he sucked in and ate two or three at a time.

Bear's thoughts drifted back to the good ole' U.S.A. and to his wife, Linda. Today was their first anniversary, and he sure missed her. Even though she was eight months pregnant, Bear bet she was out in the wheat field helping her brother and dad harvest the golden wheat grain. She was probably driving a grain hauling truck.

Bear sure missed the flat Texas Panhandle where a person could see forever, and the sunsets and sunrises were just great. The winds blew almost every day, and the air was always so clean and fresh—not like this heavy stench.

Suddenly, Bear's daydream was cut short by a radio message from the first squad's LP down the middle trail of the T - shaped trail.

"Blue Tiger 36 Delta, this is 34 Delta, over," came the whispered radio transmission.

"This is 36 Delta over."

"Bear we got two gooks coming up the middle trail on bicycles, about twenty meters down the trail from our position. They are headed your way. Are there any orders, over?"

Bear yelled to the LT and relayed the message. The LT decided to set up a hasty L - shaped ambush along the trail where the bicycle tracks were more prevalent. LT told Bear to tell the LP to let them come on through and let us know when they passed their position.

As the platoon hustled into position, Bear relayed to the LP to hold their position, let the gooks come on down the trail, and let him know when they passed.

The high Bear felt at that moment was a terrific rush. Only a person that has ever been in a life or death situation ever knows that feeling. Bear was even higher than he had been during the two Texas AAA State Championship football games at Dumas, Texas in 1961 and 1962. Boy! That seemed like a million years ago!

Bear's senses were fine tuned. He checked his M-79 grenade launcher and waited.

The platoon was in the woodline parallel to the trail that went off to the left, looking out over the chest high elephant grass and weeds.

"Bear, the two gooks just passed us, over," came the whispered transmission.

"Roger," Bear passed along the info to the LT. The platoon sergeant passed the word quickly not to fire until ordered. The plan was to try to capture the gooks first. The Kit Carson scout that was with the LRRP team would call out for the gooks to surrender.

In many cases, a Kit Carson scout was a former VC that had been repatriated to RVN.

Bear never really trusted those scouts all that much, and he always kept an eye on them.

As the two gooks came up the trail, the Kit Carson yelled in Vietnamese for them to stop and surrender. All that could be seen over the grass was their hats and black pajama - clad upper body as they pumped their bikes faster. They were about ten meters apart. They kept on moving faster and seemed to be trying to get away. Then the gook in the rear started to slow down and called out to the one in front, but the one in front started to pump faster. Bear's heart was pounding and he had a big lump in his throat.

As they turned left down the trail and were broad side to the ambush, the Kit Carson yelled again for them to stop. They both kept moving.

This all took place in a matter of minutes or seconds, but it seemed like a longer time.

"Fire!" came the order. The still jungle came alive with deafening gunfire. Bear raised his M - 79 and fired at the first rider and blew him off his bike. Bear reloaded. Both gooks were down.

"Cease fire! Cease fire!" yelled the Lieutenant.

"Hold your positions while we check out the gooks," yelled the platoon sergeant.

Bear's group, consisting of Bear, the platoon sergeant, platoon leader, Doc (the platoon medic) and the LRRP team leader, moved out to the ambush kill zone. As they approached the kill zone, Bear could here crying and the sound of movement.

Someone yelled, "They're not dead, be careful!"

As Bear came in sight to the two gooks, the mountainous high he had felt only minutes before, suddenly became a deep valley low. The first gook was lying on his back and gasping for air. The second gook was wounded also, and he was crying and attempting to hold the other one in his arms. Doc moved the crying man over to take a look at the gasping body.

Bear's heart dropped into his stomach. The gasping body was just a boy, maybe twelve years old. His chest was laid open, and Bear could see his heart beating erratically.

That far away look in his eyes would haunt Bear forever.

The boy must have belonged to the older man. The older man was forty years old or so. It was hard to tell the age of Vietnamese people because they had such a hard life and seemed to age early in life.

The older man was crying and rocking back and forth and looking at the young boy and then looking to us as if asking why.

Doc looked up at Bear and said, "Damn, Bear. He's just a kid. He won't make it. I'll give him something for the pain." Doc shot him up with morphine.

"Bear," LT said, "Tie the old man up while I call in."

Bear stammered, "But, LT."

"Do what I say, Bear, tie the gook up!"

As the LT called in, Bear removed his yellow silk scarf and tied the man's hands behind him. Doc patched up the older man's wounds. All the while the man was crying and trying to get next to the boy. His sadness overwhelmed Bear.

The platoon sergeant searched the area and the bikes and found only bamboo shoots in the bike baskets, but no weapons anywhere.

"Damn it, LT," the platoon sergeant said, "All they had was bamboo shoots!"

Bear felt even worse. What were they doing out here in the bush in a free – fire zone if they weren't VC?

Before the choppers arrived, the platoon blew up what was left of the bicycles.

Doc and Bear put the boy in a poncho to make it easier to load him in the chopper.

Finally the choppers came and the platoon sergeant popped smoke. Bear, the LRRP team, the platoon sergeant, and the two gooks loaded up in the first chopper. As Bear helped load the boy on the chopper, he could see that the boy had finally died. This world's pain was gone from the boy forever now.

As the group flew to base camp at Bien Hoa, Bear could see the platoon sergeant and The LRRP team leader discussing something. After a while the platoon sergeant moved over to Bear and said, "Bear, in order for us not to get in a big hassle, we have decided to say we found these two grenades on these gooks. Will you go with me and witness to that? Remember Bear, this is for the whole platoon. Anyway, those gooks shouldn't have been there. They may be VC. We don't know for sure."

Bear didn't know what to say, so he just told the sergeant he would think about it.

When Bear's group arrived at Bien Hoa heli-pad, they unloaded the boy's body and the older man and loaded them up in a couple of jeeps that were waiting for them. Bear and the platoon sergeant drove to Long Binh and left the boy's body for burial. They took the father to a POW camp there. By this time, the old man was very quiet and he looked very defeated. He would not make eye contact. His head was bowed.

The pair's next stop was the intelligence and investigation building where they made their report — they had found grenades on the gooks. It was easier than Bear thought it would be. Of course, the people there made it easy. Just the facts that's all.

It had started to rain as the two jeeps drove back to Bien Hoa. It rained so hard Bear could hardly see to drive, but he hardly noticed the inconvenience. Bear would always remember this day. How could he forget?

This day was his wedding anniversary. It was supposed to be a day of celebration, and it was the day he killed a boy. What a bitter taste he had in his mouth. When they got back to camp, Bear wrote the following in his diary: "Linda, I love you. Happy Anniversary. God, forgive me. I'm sorry."

FORTY DOLLARS (MPC) AND A BIBLE

MPC stood for Military Payment Certificate, and it was paid to U.S. military personnel in Viet Nam instead of U.S. currency. MPC or U.S. currency was not to be used to buy from the Vietnamese. The reason was that the rate of exchange was so much greater for MPC and U.S. currency. When it was cashed in, Vietnamese could make a lot of money. To guard against the use of U.S. currency, the soldiers were threatened with court martial. Of course, there was not much U.S. currency around because it wasn't distributed to the soldiers. On the other hand, MPC was used to purchase items quite extensively. Grunts were always ready for a good time, good food, or good drink, so, with MPC as their only money, the Vietnamese had a lot of MPC.

To combat that problem, every so often old MPC was cashed in for new MPC. Then, anyone left with the old MPC, was out of luck. It was always a surprise to the soldiers when it happened, but the gooks always knew about it a day before it happened. If you were around a heavily populated area the day before the MPC exchange was to take place, the gooks were almost giving it back to the soldiers in exchange for Vietnamese money. In some cases, the Vietnamese would strike a deal to give the soldier as much as half of the MPC if the soldier would exchange it for them.

MPC was used widely on the black market to buy and sell virtually everything. Those involved with the black market made a lot of money during the Viet Nam war.

It was the day after payday and Bear happened to have forty dollars (MPC) on him. Bear kept his money inside his little green pocket Bible. It was given to him by the Gideons at Christmas, 1967. Bear kept his pocket Bible in his left breast pocket, wrapped in plastic to keep it dry from the humidity, rain, or any water he might fall in or wade in on a mission. Bear read the Bible every chance he got, and he ended up reading it through twice during his tour of duty. Of course, sometimes he read the Bible with a beer in one hand and the Bible in the other. Surely the Lord didn't mind that a thirsty grunt was reading His word.

Right after pay call that day, the third platoon was called on a clean up mission. Bear was monitoring the radio when the message came for the platoon to saddle up. They didn't have a Lieutenant, so the platoon sergeant was in charge. Bear was his RTO that day. The mission was to be a simple one, to go out to get a body count. Some Cobra gunships had spotted a reported twenty gooks, and they had attacked them and killed several. The platoon was to be inserted from the East with a canal and woodline to the right.

Bear passed the word to the platoon sergeant and the other RTOs on the other choppers. The platoon's job was to go out and count the bodies, search the bodies for any papers or weapons, and take any prisoners if possible. A new squad of Cobra gunships and a scout chopper were to fly support overhead as the platoon accomplished its mission.

The platoon was at Di An at that time and the mission was West of Di An several miles. Bear was in the first of the three choppers. As the chopper approached the LZ and were about four feet off the ground, "Charlie" opened up fire from the woodline on the right. Bear was on the right side of the chopper. The door gunner opened up fire and deafened Bear's right ear. The pilot cut back on the throttle which was the signal for the grunts to jump off the chopper. Bear jumped off the right side, which proved to be the wrong side. Bear could see the gooks in the tree line. In fact, they were about fifty feet away from him. Bear hit and hugged the ground and fired his M-79 at the woodline.

He looked around to see where everyone else was located. The rest of the platoon was behind a rice paddy dike about one hundred feet away, firing at the gooks and yelling at Bear to get out of there. Bear never low crawled so fast in his life, radio on his back and all. Bullets bounced all around Bear and ricocheted of his radio. That one hundred feet seemed like a mile, but Bear made it in one piece. Unknowingly though, he lost his Bible and the forty bucks when his shirt pocket had come open from a button popping off. The platoon sergeant immediately got to Bear. "Bear, you okay?"

"Sure, boss, but they damn near got me."

"Call the gunships and find out their ETA."

"Roger, Sarge. Blue Tiger 36 Delta, calling Pegasus 2, over."

"This is Pegasus 2, over."

"Pegasus, we are pinned down and need your support. What is your ETA, over."

"Blue Tiger 36 Delta, our ETA is twenty minutes, over," came the reply.

"Roger, Pegasus, we'll be here, out." Bear passed the info on.

The firing had stopped and Bear peeked over the dike. Straight ahead was the canal and woodline. No movement. Maybe they had gone. In all the excitement, Bear had not even loaded his M-79 from the first round he had fired. He loaded his M-79. Bear glanced to his right. About fifty feet away were several black pajama clad bodies. The gooks hadn't left because they were trying to retrieve their dead.

"Hey, Sarge," Bear called. "Look over there to our right," Bear pointed as he called out. The platoon Sergeant acknowledged Bear.

"Bear, Smithee, and Red, you come with me," yelled the Sarge. "The rest of you lay down some cover fire."

The rest of the platoon laid down a cover fire as the four made their way to the dead VC. Bear found a U.S. Marine Corps

95

assault knife on one of the dead gooks. That was all they found on the six dead bodies. The platoon sergeant waved off the cover fire.

"Damn," Sarge said. "Where are those choppers? Okay, you all move toward the woodline!" He turned to us and said, "Okay, let's go."

The platoon reached the canal and crossed it to the woodline without any trouble. The canal was about waist deep and six feet across. They set up a circle perimeter and waited.

A scout chopper, a LOH chopper, (we called it a "mosquito chopper," because it looked so much like a mosquito) arrived first.

"Blue Tiger this is Bulldog 3 over."

"Bulldog 3, this is Blue Tiger 36 Delta, we are popping smoke." Bear said. Bear popped smoke and Bulldog 3 identified the color. This was done so the choppers would know where the good guys were located. Then the direction of fire could be directed from the smoke.

Sarge talked to Bulldog 3 and told him where to look for the VC. Bulldog 3 was armed with one M - 60 gunner and a few rockets. He skimmed over the tops of the trees following the canal system to the North of the platoon. As he started down the West tree line, a burst of machine gun fire came from the ground. The gunner fired back. Smoke came out of the chopper.

"Blue Tiger 36 Delta, we're hit! We're headed back to base. A bunker complex is located to your West," said Bulldog 3, as he flew off toward base.

Bear passed along the info and alerted the men that the gooks were to the west of them about two hundred feet. All eyes and heads turned West. Bear got on one knee and looked. He thought he saw something in the canal just West of his position.

"Get down, Bear," Sarge yelled.

"Sarge, I think I see one," Bear said as he jumped to his feet and aimed his M -79 grenade launcher toward on open area in the treeline by the canal.

What seemed like slow motion and a long time, in reality probably happened in a few seconds. Sure enough, there were two gooks wading across the canal. The one in front had his rifle over his head as he waded. The one in the rear had an RPG (rocket propelled grenade) over his head. The first gook spotted Bear.

Bear made a direct hit and both gooks disappeared into oblivion. Bear was brought back to reality by a burning sensation on his right thigh and "Doc" hollering at him.

"Bear you're hit!" Doc pulled him to the ground.

Bear's leg burned. He looked down at Doc working on his leg. Then Bear heard him say, "Bear, you're the luckiest Texan I ever saw. Those gooks ain't never going to kill you!"

Doc moved over and let Bear take a look. He had split Bear's pant leg apart at the thigh and was dabbing the wound to clean it. No, Bear wasn't going home early. It was just a piece of hot metal from his own M - 79 that broke the skin. In fact, it had quit bleeding. It just burned like a bad mat burn or scrape. Doc finished bandaging his leg. Bear reloaded his M - 79 and they all waited.

"Blue Tiger 36 Delta, this is Diamond 30, over," the call came and broke the silence.

"This is Blue Tiger 36 Delta," Bear answered.

"What's your location, Blue Tiger ?"

"We're popping smoke." Diamond 30 identified the smoke.

"Where are the Victor Charlies, over?"

Before Bear could answer, Red Horse 6, the 3/17 squadron commander came over the radio. "Blue Tiger 36, this is Red Horse 6, over" came the message. Bear nudged the platoon sergeant and said, "Sarge, Red Horse 6 wants to talk to you." Sarge took the phone.

"Red Horse 6, this is Blue Tiger 36, over."

"Blue Tiger 36, we have a large enemy force to your Northwest and headed your way. We are pulling you out. The choppers will be there shortly. Move out to the LZ and prepare to pop smoke," said the Colonel.

"Roger, Red Horse 6." Sarge turned to us."Okay men, back to the LZ and set up perimeter. We're being picked up!"

As he handed the phone back to Bear, Bear heard Red Horse 6 say, "Diamond 30, you all fly security in the area until we get this platoon out of here, over."

"Roger, Red Horse 6."

The platoon moved out to the LZ with half the platoon on one side behind the rice paddy dikes and the other by the canal. The platoon was East of their original LZ by 50 meters. Bear, Sarge, Red and Doc set up a command post around the dead VC. Everyone was nervous, waiting for the choppers. They were wondering if the large VC force would get there first. The gunships circled overhead, watching for signs of VC. From the woodline about 150 meters North of the CP all hell broke loose. Charlie had arrived.

Sarge yelled, "Bear call in the gunships."

Doc yelled "Bear take this shotgun and let me have your M -79." Doc wanted something that would shoot farther and he knew Bear was going to be busy on the radio. He was right.

Bear popped smoke and called Diamond 30 while the platoon fired at the VC.

"Diamond 30, this is Blue Tiger 36 Delta, identify smoke."

Diamond 30 identified smoke and added, "What can we do for you?"

"Diamond 30, 150 meters North of smoke is a woodline running East and West. We are receiving enemy fire at this time. Come in East to West and give'em hell!" Bear said.

"Roger, wilco," said Diamond 30. He passed along the info to the other gunships. "150 meters North of the smoke. East to West along the treeline." Two "rogers" came over the radio. Bear watched as the gunships made several passes each with rockets and machine guns blazing.

"Blue Tiger 36 Delta, this is Polar Bear 6, we are nearing your LZ for pickup, pop smoke, partner." Polar Bear 6 said.

Bear popped smoke and answered, "Roger, Polar Bear 6. Smoke popped, identify."

Polar Bear 6 identified smoke and the sorte of choppers came toward the LZ. What a relief! Bear loved those sounds of choppers coming in.

Bear passed along to Polar Bear 6, "Hot LZ, Polar Bear 6," The slicks made a pass.

"Roger, Blue Tiger. You boys read that back there?" he asked the other choppers.

"Roger," came back the reply.

Sarge shouted to the perimeter, "Okay, you guys take the first two choppers! We'll catch the third one!" Meanwhile, the gunships had silenced the woodline and headed for home, guns empty. The choppers came in with the door gunners blazing away. Bear's chopper was still moving when he mounted.

Bear jumped on the rail and fell into the chopper. The choppers started up. Bear looked out of the chopper just in time to see something at a glance. It looked familiar, Bear thought.

Zing!, a ricochet sounded, and Bear jerked his head back inside. Charlie was firing at them. The choppers banked and headed for base camp.

Suddenly, like a flash of lightning, Bear realized what it was he had seen as they took off. Oh, no! He felt of his left breast pocket. Nothing. He looked down. The button gone. His Bible and forty dollars was gone. Those damn gooks got my Bible and money, Bear thought. But, oh, the thought of no beer until next payday. Damn war, anyway.

"Say, Doc, can I borrow some money?" Bear begged.

·

EAGLE FLIGHT MISSION

The eagle circles the skies searching for its prey. Around and around the sky the great bird of prey soars scanning the ground for movement. Once the prey is spotted by the eagle's radar - like eyes, the eagle swoops in for the kill. The eagle's accuracy and swiftness are unsurpassed. The prey feels the razor - like claws dig into its skin, and then the light is gone from its life. The mission is over.

The mission was called Eagle Flight Mission. Normally the mission would consist of a few hours of flying over the jungle without much, if any, action. Several Cobra gunships would fly low and slow, searching a designated area for enemy movement, bunkers or anything that seemed suspicious. Several "Huey" choppers loaded with "grunts" (infantry men), usually a squad of eight to ten men in each chopper, would follow at a short distance, waiting to be dropped into an area to check it out after the Cobra gunships finished with the target.

Most of the time nothing would happen and the group returned to base camp. If and when the prey was spotted, each gunship would fire its rockets and machine guns and strafe the area until the Cobra felt it was okay to send in the grunts. If they expended their ammo, more Cobra gunships would be sent out to take their places to fly around for support. Sometimes artillery fire would be called in for support before or after the grunts were landed or picked up. The jungle would always be ablaze and filled with smoke.

The attack was usually swift and short, much like the eagle's attack. If the grunts were lucky, the choppers would find an LZ (landing zone) close to where the Cobras struck their prey. If not, the grunts would be set down in the nearest LZ, which would be an open area in the jungle and they would work their way through the jungle, sweeping the area for any sign of the enemy. Sometimes the small scout (LOH) choppers would be used to draw out the enemy much like the Cobras. They didn't have the fire power, but they were swift.

Most of the time it was so hot and humid, a person could hardly breathe. Humping through the bush was just plain old hard work with the added problem of "Charlie" trying to kill you, especially when you least expect it to happen. The bugs, mosquitos, and gnats constantly buzzed your head. The sweat would just soak your entire body and soak through to your ruck sack and other gear. And all the time you were humping, you knew that if you made enemy contact, it was a long way back to safety. The only comfort would be the occasional sound of the choppers as they passed overhead, circling and ready to give support. God bless those chopper pilots and crew. They were a great bunch of men.

After the mission was completed, the grunts would hump back to the LZ to be picked up. Sometimes the grunts would have a "hot" LZ. In a "hot" LZ, the enemy would be firing at the choppers as they came in to unload the grunts. In a hot LZ, the door gunners would be firing as the grunts dismounted. You never wanted to be the last off the chopper, because as the weight came off the choppers, it would rise and the last man might have a several foot drop as he dismounted. In a hot LZ, the choppers would not have a solid landing and were sitting ducks for "Charlie". They would slow down and as the rails got close to the ground, the grunts would jump out so that the chopper could get out as soon as possible. A landing was organized mayhem.

One afternoon in July, 1968 the scout squad leader and the two infantry squad leaders were called to the base camp orderly room in Cu Chi, Viet Nam. The mission was an eagle flight mission in the "Hobo Woods" Northeast of Cu Chi, the next morning at 0800 hours. There was going to be artillery support standing by, and three Cobra gunships leading the search. There would be three Huey choppers with a squad in each chopper. The men were alerted, and the grunts readied themselves, their gear, and their weapons for the mission.

But first things first. That night before, the two infantry squads were called to shore up the perimeter guard. The scout squad had a night ambush outside the wire about one half click. So went the life of a grunt. Work all night and work all day.

Bear was the RTO (radio telephone operator) for the scout squad. They slipped out of base camp about dusk. The squad reached their ambush sight along a trail and set up an L - shaped ambush. They set out their claymore mines and waited. There were two persons at each position so that while one watched the other could catch a few winks. It was one long, dark night, with no enemy contact. Every hour, on the hour, base camp would call for a radio check. The radio volume was down real low, but it always seemed so loud in the quiet darkness of the night.

"Blue Tiger 32 Delta, radio check, give two clicks on mike if all is well. Click. Click."

Just before daylight the squad gathered up their mines and headed for base camp. They grabbed a quick meal, and headed off to the waiting choppers at the chopper pad.

Three Cobra gunships led out with the three Hueys following behind, loaded with grunts. Being the RTO for the scout squad, Bear was in the lead Huey chopper. The scout squad leader was in charge of the mission on the ground.

As they lifted off, Bear went through his usual ritual. He had not been brought up in a church - going family, but he did believe in God. In his mind, he would recite the Lord's prayer and the 23rd Psalm, both of which he had learned while attending a Catholic school one year. Bear would also ask God to protect the group. Bear knew God didn't have time to fight man's wars, but maybe He would have mercy on their souls if they should not make it back.

As the choppers took off, you could see the fear of the mission in everyone's eyes. These young men, most of them still eighteen or nineteen years old, were old beyond their years. Bear was twenty- three years old and the old man of the group, and he felt at least thirty - three years old after nine months in the country. Death has a way of making a soldier old beyond his years.

As usual, the day was going to be hot and humid. As they flew out into the bush area, the heavy dew had almost burned off the bush. Viet Nam was the land of a thousand smells, and most of them reminded Bear of rotting garbage. Today was no different than usual. From the skies, the Viet Nam bush was a beautiful green country. But then the scars of war dotted the country side and were always a grim reminder of the soldier's true presence in this country.

As the choppers skimmed the tree tops, Bear monitored the radio. He listened to the Cobra pilots as they searched for a target. Their call names were White Horse six, seven, and eight. The Huey choppers were Red Dog two, three, and four. Bear's job was to monitor the radio and pass any information or instructions along to the squad leader.

Enemy movement had been reported in the area they were searching that particular day. A LRRP Recon squad had reported "boo coo" (a lot) movement. Butch, the LRRP squad leader, was fairly reliable. If he reported something, you could usually take it to the bank.

Suddenly, the radio silence was broken. "White Horse 7, did you see all those gooks?!"

"Roger, White Horse 6. Let's waste some gooks."

"Red Dog 2, this is White Horse 7, we've spotted" "boo coo" gooks. Hold your position and find an LZ (landing zone).

"Roger, White Horse 7."

"Blue Tiger 32 Delta, did you read that?"

Bear answered, "Roger."

Bear's mouth suddenly became very dry and his tongue seemed to swell up with cotton mouth. The adrenalin started flowing through his veins and his heart started pumping so hard that he could hear it in his throat and his palms began to sweat. Bear's eyes dilated to wide open. Everyone knew before Bear said anything.

"Sarge, they've spotted "boo coo" gooks. get ready to dismount."

Sarge shouted. "Okay, you guys heard him."

Sarge turned back to Bear and said, "Bear, call 33 and 34 and make sure the RTOs heard the message."

"Roger, Sarge. Blue Tiger 32 Delta to Blue Tiger 33 Delta and 34 Delta, did you all read that?" Both gave Bear a roger.

"Sarge, we're all ready."

The jungle was ablaze and filled with smoke, as the Cobras struck time and time again. The noise was deafening. Bear's fear mounted minute by minute. The "grunts" lucked out, if you could ever say that. The LZ was about two hundred meters from the target.

White Horse 7 called. "Red Dog 2, we're through for now. It's all yours."

"Blue Tiger 32 Delta, the gooks have run every which way. You all be careful down there."

"Roger, White Horse 7," Bear choked into the mike.

The ground rushed up to meet the "grunts" as they were standing on the chopper landing rails to dismount. The door gunners were blasting away with their M - 60 machine guns as the chopper approached the LZ and Bear's ears were already numb from the noise. As soon as the choppers got close to the ground, they dismounted the first chopper and set up a perimeter in the tall elephant grass.

The heat and humidity were unbearable. The second and third choppers came in and they all dismounted with no problem. The squad leaders met quickly, and the group headed for the smoking bush. Bear's squad 32, and 33 lined up on line with each man five meters apart. The 34 squad followed behind about twenty meters on line.

Bear's squad leader yelled, "Keep moving and keep each other in sight. Shoot anything that moves." The squad had gone about 100 meters when all hell broke loose on their right side. The 33 squad was getting hit pretty hard.

"32 Delta, we need support over here," yelled 33 Delta in his mike.

"Sarge, 33 needs support." Bear passed on the information.

Sarge answered, "Tell 34 to move up on line with 33 and support."

"34 this is 32 Delta. Move up on line and support 33 on our right side." Bear said.

"Roger, Bear, we're movin' up." 34 Delta answered. The bush was alive with noise and movement as the gooks rushed 33 and 34. 32 had not been hit yet, but they were ready as they held their position so as not to get ahead of 33 and 34.

Sarge yelled, "What the hell is going on, Bear?"

Bear barked into the mike, "33 or 34, what's going on over there?"

33 Delta answered, "Tell 32 we need you all over here. They're trying to flank us."

Bear relayed the message to Sarge. "Okay, men, let's swing around to the left. Let's go kill some gooks!" Sarge roared. As the squad swung around to form an "L" with the 33 and 34, they were hit from behind by "RPG" rockets. The gooks had encircled them all. 32 quickly found 33 and 34 formed a circle perimeter as best they could.

"Bear, call White Horse for support before we lose it!" Sarge ordered.

"White Horse, this is Blue Tiger 32 Delta, we need some fire power down here. We are popping smoke. We are in about a 20 meter circle around the smoke. We need a little help down here!"

White Horse identified the color of smoke and Bear acknowledged. White Horse 9 added, "Hang on to your ass down there, here we come."

The bush seemed to be one big fireball and Bear would have gotten closer to the ground, but his buttons were in the way. Bear couldn't even see who he was shooting at, but he kept firing at anything that moved or might move. After about ten minutes, which seemed like eternity, White Horse called.

"Blue Tiger 32 Delta, hey son, we're out of ammo but we'll be back"

"Roger, White Horse," "Sarge, White Horse is pulling out, they are out of ammo!"

"Let me see that radio!" Sarge said as he reached for the mike.

"Red Dog 2, this is Blue Tiger 32, pick us up at the LZ. We are coming out." Sarge said.

"Roger, Blue Tiger." said Red Dog.

"Bear," Sarge said, "Call in artillery on this position, as soon as we start to move out. Maybe we can keep "Charlie" off our ass."

Sarge shouted. "You guys, we're going back to the LZ. 32 and 33 will take the lead. 34, cover our tails."

"But Sarge," someone shouted, "We have wounded."

Sarge responded, "If we stay here, we'll all be that way. Gather up who and what you can. Don't leave anything for the gooks. Let's go."

Bear ordered into the mike, as they moved out. "Long shot this Blue Tiger 32 Delta."

"Go ahead, Blue Tiger," came the reply.

Bear gave coordinates of their position and ordered the fire mission.

"Roger, Blue Tiger, here comes the power," said Long Shot.

They saddled up and headed toward the LZ, and met no resistance. Bear could hear artillery rounds whistling overhead as the jungle exploded behind him.

Maybe they "di di moi'd" (left quick), Bear thought. The squads reached the LZ and set up a perimeter around the pick-up area. Bear popped smoke and the choppers identified the color of smoke. Man Bear was glad to hear those chopper blades slapping the air.

Sarge yelled, "33 and 34, you go first. Okay, you scouts, hang in there!" The first chopper came in and were lifting off when gunfire came from the treeline. Bear slapped his last magazine into his M - 16 and returned fire. There were gooks everywhere, Red Dog 3 came in with the M – 60's blazing, and Bear knew he had only an instant to mount up.

Bear heard a yell from behind him, and he turned to see one of his men down. Sarge, and Bear ran to him, picked him up and loaded him on the chopper. The chopper took off and they left the LZ shooting their way out as they lifted up into the sky.

It was then that Bear felt the burning sensation on his right thigh. He looked down and saw blood. Bear checked the wound. It was a flesh wound: it looked like a bullet had creased his leg. "Doc" was busy patching up the wounded while the rest of the squad checked themselves and each other.

It was quiet on the ride to base camp such a great contrast from moments before, when the sounds of explosions and human screams had filled the air. The chopper banked and swung onto the landing strip. Only then, did Bear feel a shrug of relief come over him.

As the squad unloaded, Bear started thinking, What a way to fight a war! Tomorrow D Troop would probably go back in troop force and sweep the area after the artillery and B – 52's bombard the area. Bear imagined there would be nothing left there except the bunkers and those things that couldn't be moved.

The squads made it back with everything and everyone, but they all left a little of themselves there. They had a few wounded but not bad enough to go home.

Oh, well! Where's the beer? So went the days of Blue Tiger's war.

THE GAS FRAGGING

"Fragging" was a term in Nam which meant to blow up one of your own soldiers.

In this case, CS gas grenades were used. It all started the day a whole LRRP team was wiped out by the VC at a bunker complex along a canal which was an offshoot of the Van Co Dong River, South of Cu Chi. Bear was monitoring the radio and his platoon was on red alert standby. They were working as a reactionary force in case the LRRPs needed help. It was about 1000 hours when Bear heard the extremely rushed radio message from the LRRP team leader. They had stumbled into a bunker complex and were surrounded by VC. Bear could here the firing in the background as the team leader spoke. The LRRP commander questioned the truth of the matter as he talked to the team leader. Valuable time was wasted as the Captain bickered with the team leader. It was about a thirty minute flight to the area in choppers, and another thirty minutes from the closest LZ, that was, if the platoon didn't have any trouble with the VC at the LZ.

As Bear listened to the radio, he kept thinking that the scramble horn ought to be blowing any moment. Bear warned the third platoon to get ready and that they were probably going to be scrambled to the chopper at any moment. Just before the scramble horn went off, Bear heard the last transmission from the LRRPs. The five of them were being overrun, and Bear could hear the shooting and screaming as the last word "Help" was gurgled into the radio.

The radio went dead. The red alert scramble horn went off and the third platoon loaded into the waiting chopper. Bear's scout squad boarded the first chopper and they were up and away in no time. Cobra gunships had already left and as the reaction platoon closed in on the LZ, the gunships were blowing the hell out of the area. The LZ was only large enough for one chopper at a time. The scout chopper went into the LZ first and after jumping off the chopper, the scout squad set up security around the LZ while the other two choppers came in one at a time.

After the whole unit was all on the ground, the scout squad took the point and hurried through the underbrush toward the area the LRRPs had last called in their location.

So far, they had not run into any VC, but they knew the VC were around somewhere.

The gunships had spotted some VC running away and kept blowing up the area. Bear called the Cobra gunships off the area just before his squad got to the location.

As the scout squad broke out into the small clearing, Bear spotted a bunker and called for a grenadier to fire a couple of M - 79 rounds into the bunker. The grenadier fired, but there was no return fire. The VC had apparently left the area. As the unit swept the area, they found the LRRP radio shot up and blood everywhere. Bear called that information back to the LT. The Lieutenant told him to hold up until the whole platoon could search out the area. While waiting for the rest of the platoon, Bear noticed a blood trail going toward a canal off the river. When the area had been secured by the platoon, the scout squad with the LT followed the blood trail. It appeared the bodies had been dragged, so Bear figured there was probably no hope for the LRRP team.

Bear hated being right this time.

They found their bodies. They had been stripped of everything. Their stomachs were slit open, their throats were slit, their bodies were filled full of bullet holes, and one had his genitals cut off and stuffed in this mouth. Bear had never seen such mutilation, and he couldn't comprehend this senseless slaughter. The squad dragged their bodies out and wrapped them in their rain ponchos to transport them back to the LZ. Several of the men almost puked their guts out after they found the bodies.

The platoon moved back to the LZ and were picked up and flown back to Cu Chi. As the platoon flew out of the area, artillery fire commenced on the area. "Arty" would tear up the area and one of the platoons would probably go back tomorrow for a search and destroy sweep mission.

Bear was still about half sick from finding the bodies, and riding in the chopper with the bodies made the war all the more real. What a waste! The LRRP commander could have prevented this slaughter. The more Bear thought about the day, the madder he became.

Tonight was the third platoon's night to be on stand down, which meant that they wouldn't be on ready alert standby or standby, and would probably have 24 hours off, unless they were needed on perimeter guard.

On Bear's way to his hootch, some of the other LRRPs caught him and wanted to know what had happened. Bear told them the story. The LRRPs were furious that the C.O. had left the LRRP team unprotected. Bear took a shower in cold water and went to eat at the mess hall. Then Bear went to the NCO Club to get drunk. Bear met up with some of the LRRPs and the guys from his platoon and they drank until they were all very drunk. They all tried to forget the senseless slaughter of their buddies, but the more they drank, the more their anger came boiling to the surface.

About midnight, they all made it back to one of the hootches. Some of the men wanted to "frag" the Captain to death, and Bear feared they might do it. Bear suggested that they ought to just forget about the whole thing. The Captain's hootch was a small one with doors on both ends and a real small screened area up high around the top of the building. With the doors locked, it would be pretty hard for anyone to get out.

They discussed it for a while and decided they wanted the Captain to suffer for his mistakes. They decided to throw CS gas grenades, in each end, and lock the doors, thus locking the Captain in the hootch. This wouldn't kill him, but it might send him a message. Bear tried to talk them out of it and then left to go to his hootch.

Bear watched as the others proceeded with the plan. Two of them did a recon around the hootch and returned to the others. Both doors had hasps on them and they could lock them with bolts dropped through the latch after the hasp was closed. Since the doors were solid with small screen openings on the top, they didn't think he could bust out on his own, especially with no oxygen to breathe. Two men took the East end nearest the orderly room. Two more men took positions on the other end. It was about 0200, and the SGT in the orderly room had nodded off to sleep. There was no moon and it was very dark, which added to the suspense, but Bear could still see the figures around the captain's hootch. Bear heard a short whistle. A few moments later Bear heard the doors slam, and he saw the figures run away. As they ran Bear heard the Captain yell, "What the Hell!" Then there was some coughing and hacking and then nothing.

Bear watched the spectacle. As soon as the SGT in the orderly room caught the CS smell and heard the Captain yell, he ran out of the orderly room and fell down. He was still half asleep. He jumped up and ran to the East door and tried to open it. The CS was drifting that way so he ran around to the West side. He finally figured out that the bolt was locking the door. He pulled it out and jerked the door open. He hollered into the hootch, but there was no sound.

By this time the whole West end of the hootch was crawling with soldiers. They dragged the Captain outside and tried to revive him. Apparently, he had passed out from too much gas. In the meantime, the Captain's jeep was pulled around to where he was lying. They loaded him up and took him away in a hurry. It was found out later that the captain was taken to the base hospital.

In the orderly room, the SGT hollered out to no one in particular as the jeep drove off with the Captain, "You yellow son - of - a - bitches. Come on out and I'll kick your asses."

The next morning came too early. Bear had a hangover that would kill an elephant.

It was several minutes before it dawned on him what had been done. Damn, damn, damn, he thought.

Someone yelled "Attention!" And as they all clamored to their feet and stood at attention. The LT began to speak and Bear could tell he was mad.

"Does anyone know anything about the gas grenade fragging last night?" he asked.

They all replied, "No, Sir!"

Lt said, "I want everyone to fall out in platoon formation now!"

They all hustled outside and formed up in platoon formation. The LRRPs and all the other D troop platoons formed up. They all stood at attention waiting. Bear thought to himself that damn

Captain done went and died. But the Captain didn't die, he came back to haunt them.

In a few minutes, the LRRP Captain came out of the orderly room with the D troop commander and 1st Sgt. They walked past all the units in a suspecting way. Bear thought, oh hell! Someone's going to get court - martialled. After viewing the troops, the LRRP Captain began to speak.

"Does anyone here know anything about the fragging on me last night?" he shouted.

Silence.

"Does anyone want to come forward and confess?" he shouted, again.

Silence.

"Okay, you leave me no choice. There will be two guards on two hour shifts from the stand down platoon guarding me every night from now on. And if I ever catch the soldiers who fragged me, I will personally escort them to Long Binh jail. Is that understood?" he yelled.

"Yes, Sir!!" the group answered. They were dismissed.

The Captain had made a command mistake. The fraggers had made a very serious drunken mistake. All of them would have to live with their own mistake.

It was after all not a perfect war.

WILL THE RAIN EVER STOP?

The area was III corps, War Zone D, specifically Northeast of Cu Chi in the jungles of Viet Nam. It was in August of 1968.

Bear was now a scout squad leader in the third platoon. Bear had a great squad of ten experienced men. They were closer than brothers. Nicknames were the norm. Nicknames added to comraderie. Bear was only an "acting jack" sergeant, but his squad all gave him the respect a real sergeant would demand. An "acting jack" was a soldier who wore the rank insignia and took all the responsibility of that rank but had not yet made the rank officially. Nor did he make the pay of that rank. The Army had a racket going, but "why should they buy the cow when the milk was free?"

The messenger came to Bear's tent about 0700 and let him know there was a staff meeting in the headquarters tent and announced to the squad that something was in the air, so they had better get around and eat chow and prepare their weapons and ammo.

The Lt. gave the leaders the news without any small talk. "Men, one of the LRRP squads has disappeared. The last known location was here," he said, as he pointed to the map. "We have "arty" support if we need it. You men get your maps marked and have your men draw rations and ammo for seven days. Headquarters wants us to stay out until we find them— alive or dead— and bring them in.

"The LRRP squad is Jim's bunch. There are five of them and one Kit Carson (Vietnamese scout). We will set down in the LZ close to where they last reported in and move from there to the first resupply point and checkpoint. From there, nobody knows until we get there. We leave at 1000 hours. Bear, your scout squad will be in the first chopper and take the point once we are on the ground. The second squad will take the rear chopper and be the rear guard. Myself and the platoon Sergeant will be with the first squad in the middle chopper. The first squad will handle the headquarters security and the flank security. We will have a Vietnamese scout with us by the name of Ben. Any questions?"

Everyone shook their heads no and they all left. Bear went directly to his squad's tent. "Okay, you heroes," Bear said as he entered the tent, "listen up. We have a LRRP team to find and we're not coming back until we find them, so pack your rucksacks accordingly. We leave at 1000 hours. Draw your rations and ammo. I'll be back at 0930 to assemble and you all better be ready."

"Sarge, you reckon we'll get K rations for this mission?" asked Mouse. Mouse was a small man, hence the name Mouse. He was the tunnel rat, the man who checked out the tunnels they found.

"Mouse, I have no idea, but doubt it. Besides, when was the last time the Army did what you thought it should?"

"Never!" someone answered. Everyone chuckled.

"My point exactly," Bear said as he left the tent. Bear was more right than he wanted to be because they got "C" rations. "K" rations or what was called "LRRP" rations, consisted of freeze-dried food in waterproof pouches. They were light weight and soldiers could carry a lot more food. A "grunt" only had to add water to make a meal. "C" rations were heavy, bulky cans of food.

When the squad had "C" rations, they took the small tins of peanut butter, cheese, crackers, coffee, sugar, hot cocoa, and cigarettes. From the large cans they would eat all that they could stand and hide the rest of the food in their tents for later. Besides they were supposed to be resupplied with water, food, and ammo at the first checkpoint and that should take about three days. When and if they found the LRRP team, they could be back sooner. The scuttlebutt was that the LRRP team had reported enemy movement last evening from the first checkpoint and had not been heard from since.

It was the rainy season in Nam, and the weather was unpredictable. A hard driving rain storm could pop up in the wink of an eye. Six inches of rain could fall in a matter of minutes. As always, this day was a little overcast and very humid. It had been raining very recently. Bear packed his rucksack for the long haul with lots of ammo, rain poncho, wool blanket, extra wool socks, and a towel. Bear knew he would get wet eventually in the monsoon rains, but it was better to be wet and warm than wet and cold. The wet wool could keep a grunt warm as if in his Mother's womb, but if the wind blew, you could still get chilled. The wool worked like insulation for your body.

Bear mounted the PRC - 25 radio on his rucksack. His squad was understrength so he didn't have the luxury of a RTO. Bear carried his own radio quite often. He had gained plenty of experience as the LT's RTO and besides that, he wanted as many riflemen as he could get to fight. An RTO was not much more than a pack animal at times. He had to carry everything that everyone else did, plus the radio. At times the RTO was too busy on the radio to do much fighting. There were many times when Bear shucked the radio in order to fight. Bear felt that if someone had to carry the extra load, it might as well be him.

Bear ate some "C" rations while he packed and thought of home, which seemed so very far away, like in another universe or another time. Bear had heard of the turmoil back in the U.S.A.. He couldn't understand why people protested the U.S.A. helping a country protect itself from communism. If only those Americans would support the troops, the war could be won.

Bear assembled his squad at 0930 and checked them out thoroughly. They were ready as always. They all knew what to expect. A green recruit usually didn't know what to expect and he might pack a lot of unnecessary items. When you have to carry your world around in your rucksack on your back, you find out real quick which things are really necessary and important for your survival. And survival was the name of this game.

Bear had given up on winning the war this year. He just wanted to make it home alive.

At 1000 hours they loaded onto the waiting choppers and headed out to the LZ. The platoon landed with no problem. The sound of a chopper leaving you out in the boonies was always a very frightening feeling, like cutting your life line. The platoon was on "Charlie's" turf now where there was no place to run and no place to hide.

The platoon assembled, and after the leaders met, Bear took his squad on point. They headed toward their destination —

checkpoint #1. Bear rotated the point man every thirty minutes or so to keep the point man alert. Everyone got his turn on point, even Bear.

Why should he be any different? The job was extremely important. A good alert point man might mean the difference between walking into a death trap and survival.

The platoon avoided the main trail like the plague because of the danger of booby traps and ambushes, so the going was very slow. The area they were in was a light jungle area with lots of open areas and small undergrowth. The ground was saturated and water stood in the low spots. It was like being in a swamp at times. The leeches were terrible and they seem to drop out of the sky. The continuous drone of the gnats and mosquitos was almost maddening. Within a few hours they were all drenched in there own perspiration.

The platoon moved onward until about dusk, making about 500 hundred meters. They set up camp in a wide circle in a small grove of trees that afforded them good visibility in all directions. The platoon set out their claymore mines, and the command post was put in the center of the encircled group. There were two men at each position and one of the men was to be awake at all times. Each position was within twenty feet of each other and visible to each position on either side of them.

After the area was secured, they ate. Grunts cooked with C - 4 explosives because it made a very hot, smokeless fire. With a small chunk of C - 4, a person could boil up a canteen cup of water for cocoa or coffee in a matter of minutes. If it wasn't available, the back of a claymore mine could be pried off and the C - 4 inside the mine could be used. Bear always kept a chunk of C - 4 in his rucksack for cooking. Bear didn't think the "big boys" would have approved, but what the hell, they weren't living out here like animals either.

"Sarge, LT wants to pow wow with all the squad leaders at the CP (command post) in ten minutes," said the LT's RTO.

"Roger that", Bear said. Bear finished eating and went to the CP. It was dark and cloudy. You couldn't see your hand in front of your face or your butt dragging along behind.

The LT reminded the leaders to keep their men alert and quiet. If anyone fired a weapon, there had damn well better be a body or he was in trouble. Anyone giving our position away with some silly behavior would be court martialled. The platoon had three green kids with them, and the LT reminded the leaders to give them special attention and match them up with an experienced hand. There would be no LPs (listening posts) or ambushes sent out tonight because the platoon wanted to remain inconspicuous. The Lieutenant didn't think "Charlie" knew they were here yet. They all hoped so.

It was a long, dark, boring night, one of those nights when ten minutes seemed like an hour. It was quiet all night — almost too quiet for comfort. It sprinkled on the platoon off and on all night, but they didn't have a major rainstorm. But the way the clouds were building and moving, Bear expected a flood. The best thing that happened that first night was that there was no "Charlie".

The platoon broke camp the next morning after they ate, and continued through the swampy jungle. About noon things started to happen. The point man spotted a squad of VC headed in the platoon's direction. Bear called the LT to report and was told that the orders at this time were to remain unseen as possible so that they might have a better chance of finding the LRRP team. The platoon all hid in the bush and waited quietly. The gooks passed by at a distance without incident. From the platoon's position they couldn't see the VC but they could hear them. They platoon was edgy as they waited patiently.

LT called in the platoon's location, and reported the gooks and the direction they were going. Artillery command, unknown to LT., thought they were suppose to fire a few rounds of artillery. Before the platoon could start their movement, the first rounds came whistling overhead and blew the jungle to smithereens. The platoon all hugged the ground as pieces of the world fell all over them. Bear almost wet his pants, primarily because he didn't know that it was his own artillery. For all Bear knew, the VC had spotted the platoon and all hell was going to break loose.

Bear called LT. "What's going on LT?"

"I don't know Bear, but I'll damn sure find out!" answered LT. After a few minutes LT called us back, "It's okay, you guys, it's our own stuff. Some trigger happy SOB decided to keep Charlie honest. Let's move out."

Bear took his turn on point. As the unit moved out, it started raining and lightning. It seemed that with every step Bear took, the rain came down harder and the lightning got closer. They had been progressing fairly slow, and with the rain they were even slower. Bear could hardly see where he was going half the time. They all got soaked and chilled to the bone as the wind blew. Before long the jungle floor was covered with several inches of water. Sometimes, it seemed it rained leeches because leeches were on the underbrush and soon they were on the grunts. Bear hated those leeches. When they started sucking the blood, you would feel a sting like a wasp sting. If you caught them just in time, you could pull them off. Otherwise, if they were already latched - on, the only thing you could do was burn them until they let go. The only problem with burning them now was that it was to wet to burn anything. Mosquito repellent would sometimes work, but it also burned from the wound.

Bear figured they were going nowhere fast. LT decided to stop and set up a perimeter and wait out the storm. Bear dropped his rucksack and got out his wool blanket and put it over him to try to create a little warmth. As he huddled in the bush, the rain seemed as if it might last forever. They set up in groups of two. One watched while the other one ate and napped. In a while, Mouse and Bear switched roles. Bear covered his head with his poncho to form a small tent, broke out his P -38 (can opener), and opened some peanut butter and had peanut butter and soggy crackers. The platoon was in a low spot and the water was six inches deep before long.

There was no place to go so the platoon just watched and got soaked. It seemed they were there for an eternity, but it was actually just a few hours. Finally it quit raining, but the wind kept blowing and made it ever so cold. Bear hated to get out of his cozy tent but duty called. When the rain let up, the platoon continued on their way. But now they were wading through the bush. Bear hated this job. What a way to live! or Die!

The platoon had been on the move for a short time when the unmistakable sound of an AK - 47 broke the silence. Three shots rang out from nowhere. One of the men was hit in the shoulder. "Medic!", Bear hollered. Someone yelled, "It's a sniper up there in the tree!" As he let out a burst with his M - 16, and one gook tumbled to the ground.

"Bear, hide the body", LT said over the radio. Bear got two of his men to hide the body. Bear knew every VC in the area was alerted now, so they needed to get out of this area pronto. Doc patched up Ben, the Vietnamese interpreter. The bullet was still in Ben's shoulder, and it was a very nasty wound. The greatest two dangers was from infection or internal injuries.

"You're going to be okay, Ben." Bear said, as he helped him to his feet.

"I know Bear," Ben answered in broken English.

Doc called Bear aside and told him that someone should carry Ben's gear and his rucksack because he needed to conserve his strength. Ben was in a lot of pain especially when any pressure was put on the shoulder area. Doc continued reminding everyone about watching for signs of infection.

Doc told the platoon leader, "We need to get Ben a medi - vac as soon as possible."

"Okay, Doc," We'll get him out at the first checkpoint. We should be there tomorrow sometime."The Lieutenant agreed that he would get Ben out as soon as possible. Infection and / or gangrene could turn a small wound into a death sentence in this nasty quagmire. Besides the wound seemed to be more internal and Ben could be bleeding to death.

The platoon continued for a while longer and set up their circle perimeter for the night. The circle was closer together and not as large tonight, for they had to put out LPs to keep from getting any surprises from "Charlie". An LP consisted of a couple of men with a radio sent out a short way from the perimeter to watch and listen. They would call in every hour to report. LP was lonesome duty and the possibility of getting cut off from the main group was tremendous. You could say that the LP was out on the very end of the limb and could be cut off at any time.

About midnight the rain and lightning started up again. It was a miserable night and seemed eons long. Between the rains, the bugs kept the grunts even more miserable. By daybreak it had quit raining but the wind made it seem as cold as a fall football night in the Texas Panhandle. Bear heated some water in his canteen cup for hot cocoa, and ate some cheese and wet crackers. Bear lit a cigarette after he ate. Bear had never smoked until he came to Nam. He smoked out of nervousness. He really didn't like it that much. Now a chew of tobacco or a good cigar was another story altogether.

The LT called a meeting at the CP when the platoon was about ready to move out.

"Bear, you need to take half of your squad and get Ben to the first checkpoint for dust - off by noon. Doc tells me that Ben's wound is getting worse. You all can move faster with a smaller group. I have already called for a chopper. Maybe we can beat the next rain storm that is predicted. We will be right behind you. Report back when you make it to the #1 checkpoint LZ, and I'll call the chopper. Good luck," said LT.

"Yes, sir..." Bear said as he left the CP. "Okay, men, listen up! You three and Ben will go with me. We are going on ahead to the LZ to secure it and get Ben out of here. We are moving as fast as we can. The rest of you will answer to Mouse. Mouse, keep moving like we have been moving. Okay let's move out."

The five men moved out toward the LZ. The scout squad had divided up Ben's equipment among them, so that no one man would be overloaded. Ben was getting weaker by the minute, as his body fought the infection. The sun had come out and it was very humid. Every breath contained more water than air. Two years ago Bear had played college football at 235 lbs., but now he weighed around 185 lbs.. This bush could suck the life right out of you. Bear had developed a sore throat from just being wet and cold. He could only imagine how Ben felt.

Bear's group moved as fast as Ben could move with frequent stops. They had to get to checkpoint LZ before it started raining again so that the choppers could fly. The choppers couldn't fly in a driving rain. They flew in pretty bad weather, but the way it had been raining they would never find the LZ.

143

About noon Bear's group approached the LZ. It was an oblong area about 50 x 100 meters, with three trails entering and leaving the area. Chest high elephant grass occupied the open area so it would be easy to stay out of sight until they had to load Ben on the chopper. Bear got Ben secured and they all spread out to check the area. After the area was secured, Bear called the LT.

"Blue Tiger 36, this is 32, over."

"Blue Tiger 36, over",

"36, we have secured the first checkpoint. We are ready for the dust - off. No sign of the LRRP team, over", Bear said.

Roger, 32, I'll call the dust - off and resupply choppers. We should be at your location in a couple of hours, over."

"Roger, 36, out.

Bear and his men continued to search the area for signs of the LRRP team, but the rain had washed away all evidence. In this thick bush, a person might pass right by a body and not see it. If they were dead, you would be able to smell their bodies long before you might spot them. But Bear was being negative — he should have been thinking positive, that they would find them all alive.

They all met back where they had stashed Ben. Now all they had to do was wait and watch — something a grunt in Nam had a lot of experience doing. A bad storm was brewing and they could see it and feel it in the air. Bear hoped they could get Ben out of there before the storm hit, or he might not make it. Bear changed his bandage and the wound did not look so good. In fact, it was infected. The wound was a greenish - black color around the edges, and Bear knew gangrene had started. The smell was bad, too. Bear consoled Ben as best he could, but he felt helpless because all he could do was wait.

The sound of a heavy fire fight split the silence and alerted Bear to the fact that the war was still on. From the way it sounded, with the AK - 47s firing a lot at first, it sounded like the rest of the platoon had been ambushed.

"Blue Tiger 36, this is Blue Tiger 32, over," Bear said. Nothing. Bear repeated the message twice more. Silence. Finally,

36 answered. Bear could hear the firing and yelling over the radio as LT talked. "36, do you want us to pull back and lend a hand?"

"Negative, 32. Hold your position. I'll let you know when we move out so you will know when to expect us, over."

"Wilco and out."

Bear listened to the fight and he could tell the platoon was not too far away. The rain started falling down and it was a gully washer. It was late afternoon by now, and Bear figured the choppers were not coming. After an hour or so the battle stopped. The rain poured down in bucket size drops. If it would only stop raining, Ben might make it out alive.

"Blue Tiger 32, this is 36, over." LT said to Bear over the radio. "Bear the choppers are not coming, We are staying here until the rain stops. "Charlie" hurt us pretty bad. You all stay where you are. I will let you know when we start moving up to your position. Keep in radio contact tonight. You all have a nice night, out."

"Roger, 36, same to you."

Bear told his men. Their stares told him how disappointed they were. They were on edge and exhausted. It would be a long night once again. Bear ate the last of his tins of peanut butter and cheese with the last of the soggy crackers. Bear washed it down with cold water coffee.

Bear set up in a position where each soldier could cover each others backs. About midnight, Ben got the chills. He had a fever but he was shivering. Bear got under Ben's blanket and poncho with him for the added warmth. Bear used his blanket to wrap Ben even more. Bear put his OD (Olive Drab) Army color towel over his head and stared out into the cold, rainy darkness.

"Bear, will the rain ever stop?" Ben asked, as he shook uncontrollably.

"I don't know. I wish I knew. I'm sure it will, eventually, Ben."

No one could see Bear's tears as they mixed with the rain running down his face. Nobody ever told him war was like this. Bear knew Ben might not make it now. He prayed silently — Lord, give Ben rest.

Toward daybreak, the rain stopped and the sun came up. Bear was afraid to move to check Ben since they were warm. Bear did not want to disturb Ben, and he was quiet anyway. Day broke with the welcome sun shining. The gnats, mosquitos, and various other bugs were already swarming Bear and his men. Bear had never been so miserable.

"Ben, the rain stopped." Bear said, as he nudged him. But Ben did not move. The rain had stopped for Ben forever. His suffering was over. The lump in Bear's throat and the tears in Bear's eyes told the other men Ben's fate. Bear did not have to say a word.

They all knew Ben was dead.

They all sat staring at each other, not knowing what to say or do. Finally, Bear broke the silence, "Let's scout the area before the choppers arrive." The pain they all felt had to be suppressed for now. Although Ben was a Vietnamese, he was a friend.

Bear and his men scouted the area again to make sure "Charlie" didn't have a surprise waiting for the choppers. They found nothing. Bear finally got some C - 4 lit and made hot water for hot cocoa.

"Blue Tiger 32, this is 36, over," the radio barked.

"This is 32, over," Bear said.

"32, we're moving out to your location. Be alert for us coming in. Resupply and dust - off are on their way to the LZ."

"Roger, 36,", "Okay men, let's spread out around the LZ," Bear ordered. Bear pointed out their positions. Bear stayed around the area where the platoon should arrive.

After a little over an hour, the platoon linked up with Bear's group. Shortly thereafter, the choppers arrived. Bear popped smoke to guide them to the LZ. The choppers unloaded the resupply. Bear loaded Ben into his poncho and they carried him to the chopper. Then the wounded were loaded on the chopper.

The platoon set up around the outside of the whole LZ and rested and ate and cleaned their weapons. Meanwhile, leaders divided up the ammo and food. "C" rations again, but man it was great. They all ate like ravenous wolves, and packed the rest in their rucksacks. They buried the empties and boxes in the sloppy mire.

The platoon waited for orders from base camp. They were to give the platoon their next checkpoint. Base camp sent the orders to sweep the whole area about 200 meters around our present LZ checkpoint #1, after which the platoon was to proceed to checkpoint #2. LT decided to divide the platoon up into three squads and each squad would be responsible for various sectors. Bear relayed the orders to his men. The platoon kept in close radio contact.

It had been hot and humid, but as the storm clouds gathered it became cooler, and Bear knew it was going to pour rain again soon.

Bear saddled up his squad and they moved out to their sector. Their sector was a low area which meant it would be wet and sloppy. Bear brought his squad on a straight line within sight of each other, and they moved forward to search the area.

The rain poured, the squad had a hard time keeping each other in sight. Within an hour, they were knee - deep in nasty water, wading toward their goal. Damn, this country stunk or was it Bear's body odor? Even the bugs and mosquitos didn't bother Bear now because he smelled so bad. On the first sweep, they found nothing, and Bear called the LT to report.

"36, this is 32, over."

"Go ahead, 32."

"36, we are ready to move over and start our sweep back. We haven't found anything, over."

"Negative, 32 the first squad found one of the LRRPs bodies in his sector. We will all head back to the following coordinates."

The platoon leader read the coordinates. Bear had a quick pow wow, and they headed back through the driving rain. As they approached the checkpoint #1 LZ area, Bear spotted movement and heard gooks talking. Bear set his squad up in a hasty ambush along one of the trails.

"36, this is 32, over," Bear said.

"36, over,"

"36, we got gooks in checkpoint #1 area, we are set up in an ambush, over."

"Roger, 32, trigger the ambush when you are ready, over."

"Roger, 36," Bear signaled the men to fire on his signal. The rain was still falling hard. They had to wait until the VC patrol was very close because of the rain.

Bear thought to himself, "Come on gooks, just a little closer." Finally, Bear triggered the ambush. The six gooks didn't know what hit them. The squad searched the bodies and stripped them of their weapons. They hid the bodies in the treeline and continued on their way. The going was slow because the ground was so wet and muddy. Their vision wasn't too great either. About dark Bear's squad linked up with the other squads and set up their positions around the command post.

"Tonight, we will send out a small ambush patrol further along the trail where the LRRP body was found. Bear, take four of your men and set up the ambush," LT. said.

Roger that, "Sir." "Shoot to kill, Bear. "Charlie" already knows we're around here. If you get in trouble, come back inside the perimeter. Radio check every hour, Bear. Call before you come in, and good luck."

"Yes, Sir."

By the time Bear's squad left to set up their ambush, the rain had let up some. It was so dark that Bear couldn't see his hand in front of his face. They set up their ambush back - to - back in a fork of the trail so they could see all directions. Two would nap while two watched. They were all dead tired. Bear didn't know how they kept going. Bear's sore throat was real bad now, and he had no energy. Bear had also developed a bad case of crotch rot, commonly known as jock itch. His inner thighs were raw. The thought of "Charlie" slitting his throat was all that kept him awake on his watch.

At this stage of the mission, the platoon was all operating on pure instinct. They had no concept of time or the rest of the world. They were all they had to keep each other alive. Bear felt so close to these guys even though he could not tell you much about some of them or even what some of their full names were. In the Nam, you operated on nicknames. Things were simpler that way because you never knew who would be alive tomorrow.

The rain quit about daylight, but the start of the day was very foggy. The air was so wet that Bear's lungs felt like they had water in them.

Bear's squad linked up with the platoon and ate what breakfast they had. Peanut butter, and soggy crackers with hot cocoa made up Bear's breakfast. He thought that when he got home to the U.S.A., he was going to sleep and eat all he wanted to for thé rest of his life. Bear's mind played tricks on him, for he couldn't remember whether this was the fourth or fifth day out — maybe even longer. He had lost all sense of time.

The LRRP body they had found had been mutilated. It was hard to imagine that this body was a live person at one time. It seemed so unreal. "Charlie" loved to either decapitate a body or cut the genitals off the body and stick them in the mouth. "Charlie" would also gut a body by slitting the belly so the guts would show. This LRRP body was gutted. That sight was always a grim reminder of the ever present cruelty and death around.

The leaders met and the Lieutenant mapped out their destination parallel to the most worn path where the LRRP body had been found. They were to sweep this area to checkpoint #2. Bear's scout squad would lead the way again. After Bear briefed his men, they headed toward their destination. Bear knew they were all hoping that this would be where they would be extracted and taken back to base camp. Bear could sense that in everyone.

By the middle of the afternoon, it was partly sunny and hot and very humid. They made good time — too good because the point man got careless and walked right into a VC ambush. "Charlie" let Bear's squad through before they sprung the ambush so as to separate them from the other squads. The ambush was a good one for "Charlie" because the platoon was surprised. "Charlie" seemed to come out of the woodwork. There were gooks everywhere. These were NVA regular soldiers, and they had the fire power.

"Bear, this is 36, over," LT said.

"32, over,"

"Bear, take your squad and secure the LZ at checkpoint #2. We're going to run for it when we call arty on our position."

"Roger that, 36." Bear gathered his squad and they practically ran to the LZ as the battle raged behind them. They made a quick sweep and set up a perimeter and waited for the rest of the platoon. Bear was low on ammo, as was everyone else. The rest of the ammo had to count. The sky rumbled with thunder. Bear prayed, "Lord, don't let it rain 'til we get out of here."

Bear heard the artillery explode the bush in a billion pieces, and he knew the platoon would be coming soon.

"Blue Tiger 32, this is 36, over," Bear heard the LT on the radio.

"32, over."

"The choppers are on the way to checkpoint #2 LZ."

"Roger, 36," Bear replied.

"Okay, you all be alert," Bear said to his squad, "Don't shoot any of our guys."

Bear no more than got it out of his mouth when the rest of the platoon started coming out of the bush to his position. Bear could hear the firing as the rear guard covered the others' escape. The platoon leader had a quick staff meeting. They organized the perimeter guard just in case they had to spend the night. Then the Lieutenant gave them the bad news.

"Men, we had to leave the dead LRRP behind. We'll come back for him later." His voice faltered as he made the last statement. They all knew that he might be lost in the bush forever.

And then the rain came down in a torrential downpour. The rear guard arrived at the LZ.

"Blue Tiger 36, this is White Horse 3, over," came the transmission on the radio.

"This is Blue Tiger 36, over," Bear could hear the LT say.

"Blue Tiger 36, we're scrubbing our mission. It's raining too hard. Sorry, guys. Good luck," came the reply.

"Roger, White Horse, 36 out." The disappointment in his reply said it all for all of them.

It rained and rained. Bear had no food left. he was soaked. He was cold. Damn war anyway, he thought. What the hell is this all about?

Darkness came early as the rain kept falling hard.

Bear pulled his Marine assault knife out that he had taken from a dead gook a few months back and stabbed it in the mud beside him. Bear had two M - 16 magazines left — about 36 rounds. A knife and two grenades and 36 rounds between life and death. The night crawled by at a snail's pace. It rained until about 4 a.m., and then the wind blew hard to chill the soldiers already soaked bones. By daybreak it was raining again. Bear remembered Ben's dying words, "Will the rain ever stop?" as the rain soaked his already saturated body. Bear felt like dying. Maybe the pain would go away then.

Either "Charlie" couldn't find the platoon or the arty had hurt him bad for there was no more contact. Early afternoon the sun broke out of the clouds a little, and the platoon all hoped they were getting out of there soon.

The long silence was broken by the radio transmission. "Blue Tiger 36, this is White Horse 3, over."

"Blue Tiger 36, over," LT answered.

"You grunts ready to go home?"

"Roger that for sure."

"Well, pop smoke, we're almost there."

LT's RTO popped smoke. The chopper jock identified smoke. Anticipation swelled up inside of Bear until he thought he would explode. Come on, hurry up!

An NVA patrol spotted the smoke too and started firing at the platoon.

LT called White Horse 3, "Victor Charlie's just arrived, we have a hot LZ. I repeat, a hot LZ."

"Roger that, 36," White Horse 3 said. "We're coming in with blazing guns. Keep your heads down."

Bear emptied one magazine. One magazine left. Bear thought, I'll save it for the run to the chopper. The beautiful sound of the choppers flying in to the LZ, firing away, sounded like music to Bear. They all ran toward the choppers and mounted quickly. The door gunners sprayed the treeline with their M – 60's. Bear was deafened by the sound. He thought to himself, hurry let's get out of here, and breathed a sigh of relief when they were finally airborne.

Bear dozed off for a few minutes, but he awakened with a start when he thought he heard Ben say, "Bear, it stopped raining." The realism of the dream scared him. The tears welled up in Bear's eyes and a lump swelled in his throat. He choked them down, and held back the tears. But his heart ached.

It was great to get back to base camp. They all passed out from exhaustion. The next day two companies from the First Infantry Division went out and retrieved the dead. They never found any more LRRP team bodies. They met with little enemy contact. As always, the VC and NVA had left the area.

VULTURE FLIGHT

If you know anything about vultures or buzzards, you know that they circle around an area where something dead is located. After making sure it is dead, they pick the carcass clean. A vulture flight mission was essentially the same principle. Choppers would circle an LZ at several thousand feet and watch the F – 15's strafe the area and drop their bombs and then watch the gunships fire their loads on the LZ. Then the choppers with the troops in them would swoop down into the burning smoking LZ to check it out and to pick it clean.

On this day, the platoon was up at 0400. B –52's had bombed the area of operation most of the night, making it hard to sleep with the noise and the vibration from the bombs. A large VC unit area had been discovered by the LRRP unit of whom D Troop was attached. Artillery fired into the area just prior to the unit leaving Cu Chi for the HoBo woods area. The platoon ate breakfast at 0500 and double checked their gear. At 0700 the platoon moved out to the waiting helicopters.

Bear was the scout squad leader, and his squad was in the first chopper. This was a platoon - size mission. The platoon had about twenty men available for this mission, so they were only using three choppers. The VC unit had been estimated as a battalion - size unit. Bear never understood why the army sent an under strength platoon after a battalion - size VC unit and possible bunker complex, but their job was not to question higher up command. Bear guessed command figured that they spent all that ammo blowing the hell out of the area, so there shouldn't be any enemy left.

The platoon flew out of Cu Chi and the choppers climbed higher than they usually did on regular missions. Bear looked out the door of the chopper and the ground looked so very far away and the trees were so small they almost didn't look real.

As they neared their destination, the choppers were, what seemed like several thousand feet in the air, and Bear could see the LZ area on fire and smoking. As the choppers began their circling of the area like vultures, the F - 15 fighter jets had arrived and were making their runs on the LZ area. There were three jets, each taking turns pelting the area with their loads. The pilots would climb up and around after their individual run and prepare to make another dive - bombing run. The pilots would dive toward the LZ area from several thousand feet up in the air and just about the time you thought they would crash into the ground, the pilots would pull up and skim the tree tops as they sprayed the area with their machine guns and dropped their various bombs.

The fighters dropped napalm, high explosives, and cluster bombs. The napalm had the jungle on fire. The cluster bombs exploded and spread further explosions around the jungle. The platoon watched from the circling choppers as the fighter jets made many runs until they exhausted their ammo. Bear carried his own PRC - 25 backpack radio since his regular RTO had gone on R & R. Bear listened to the chatter among the three pilots. They said they had taken on small arms fire and had even seen VC scampering around. How could anyone still be alive? The area was peppered with the B - 52 bomb holes from last night's bombing. It was unbelievable that anyone could still be alive.

Bear passed the word on to his squad that this would be a hot LZ. It had been decided that all three choppers would go into the LZ together and secure the LZ together, since Bear only had five men in his squad. Normally, the scout squad would have a dozen men and they would go into the LZ first, and secure the perimeter for the rest of the platoon to come in to the LZ.

After the fighters finished, the choppers banked and they dropped toward the LZ. As they approached the tops of the trees, Bear noticed that four Cobra gunships were circling and firing into the woodlines for support and protection. The door gunner on Bear's side of the chopper opened up with his M - 60 and Bear's ears became deaf from the noise. As soon as the runners were ten feet above the ground, Bear stepped down on the landing rails ready to jump off onto the ground.

From the woodline, Bear heard the distinct AK - 47 sound as the VC fired at the chopper. Bear tried not to notice the bullets ricocheting off the chopper. The squad was motioned by the door gunner to get off the chopper. The chopper was a foot from the ground, which wasn't far considering they were taking on VC fire.

Bear hit the ground running away from the chopper and fired into the woodline.

After his squad got about half - way to the tree line, they hit the ground and waited for the platoon leader to contact them. Bear and his men choked on the smoke from the burning jungle. The LZ had four - foot - tall "elephant" grass and the humidity and heat near the ground were stifling. The dry grass was on fire in several places around the LZ, and the smoke was choking everyone. Bear pulled his yellow silk scarf over his mouth and nose so he could breathe easier.

"32—36 over," the LT called.

Bear answered, "32, over."

"Bear take your squad toward the East side of the LZ and when you secure the area, call us."

"Roger, 36." Bear gathered his squad into his position and told them the orders.

Bear got the squad on line and they leap - frogged forward to the edge of the tree line.

Two would move up as the other three covered them, and then vice versa, until they reached the trees.

A trail headed on East through the jungle with a bunker facing the squad. Just to be safe, Bear had a M - 79 grenade fired into the bunker. There was no reply, so the squad moved on into the jungle. They spread out and secured the area. Bear called the LT and told him they were ready for them to move to their position. LT called back that as soon as the "Dustoff" came in for the two wounded, they would move up. From what Bear gathered on the radio, two men had gotten into punji stake pits and needed medical attention. The "dustoff" came in and took off with the wounded a couple of minutes after Bear talked to LT.

When the rest of the platoon arrived, the LT informed them all that they would circle the LZ and gradually widen their circle as they continued around the LZ. The platoon was to get a body count, and blow - up what they could with the C - 4 explosives they had with them. The larger bunker complexes, if any, would be blown - up by the demolitions engineer group that would come in later.

Bear assembled his squad and they started their sweep three abreast, just far enough away from the open LZ area to still see it. The squad kept each other in sight and moved around the LZ area. They had moved only a couple hundred meters when they came under fire from a bunker complex. Bear called the LT to let him know what was going on. He hit the ground and almost landed in a punji pit. He uncovered the pit and dropped a grenade in it as he rolled away from the pit. Bear moved the second line of three up on line with the first line and had the M – 79's fire at the bunker. Two M – 79 rounds were a direct hit.

As soon as the VC return fire stopped, the squad moved up and checked out the bunker. There were two VC bodies in the bunker itself, and a blood trail that headed off into the jungle. By this time the rest of the platoon had gotten to their position. While the rest of the platoon checked out the immediate area, Bear took one man he called Runt, with him to check out the blood trail.

Runt was the platoon tunnel rat. After grenades were dropped in the tunnel entrance, Runt would be lowered into a tunnel by a rope, with a pistol and flashlight and ear plugs, to search out the tunnels.

Bear and Runt followed the blood trail to a series of spider holes. Spider holes were foxholes camouflaged and the top covered over with a solid - type lid for the VC to hide in. Sometimes the spider holes would be at an entrance to a tunnel complex. They blew up several spider holes before they found one where the blood trail ended. Bear motioned for Runt to pull the pins on two grenades, and as he did so and counted to three seconds, Bear flipped the lid with his rifle barrel. Runt popped the grenades in the hole. You always pulled the pins and counted to three to keep the VC from tossing the grenades back at you.

The two grenades blew the hell out of the hole. When the smoke cleared, they discovered an entrance to a tunnel. Bear popped a CS gas grenade down in the tunnel entrance to flush out the VC. Sometimes a gas or smoke grenade would lead you to other entrances to a tunnel complex when you would see the gas or smoke come out of other places. Sometimes the gas grenade would flush out the VC. They waited for a few minutes, but nothing happened.

Bear called the Lieutenant on the radio and told him what he had found. The Lieutenant told Bear to prepare Runt to go in the tunnel as soon as the gas was gone.

Very suddenly, a gook jumped out of a spider hole about twenty meters from Bear and started running away. They both fired and the VC dropped. They went to check out the body and the spider hole where the VC had come from. Bear rolled the VC over. It was a woman. She had no weapon but she did have a pouch filled with medical supplies. This was probably the hospital area of the tunnel complex. That spider hole was another entrance to the tunnel complex.

The platoon leader called on the radio that he had found another tunnel entrance.

Bear told him of his find. The second entrance was large enough for Bear to go inside, if he left his radio outside the hole. The platoon leader arrived at Bear's position about the time the two were going inside the tunnel. Bear told him he was going with

Runt and showed LT where the other entrance was located. LT quickly sent two "grunts" to cover the other entrance.

The entrance quickly opened up into a large underground mess hall or classroom structure. It was so large, Bear could stand up in the room. The room was filled with tables and benches (handmade from the jungle,) Bear couldn't go any further because the tunnel became too small for him.

Runt, with his pistol, ear plugs, and flashlight continued on into the tunnel. The tunnel led to the first spider hole tunnel they had found. The reason Bear knew that was because he could here Runt tell the men guarding the hole not to shoot, that it was Runt and he was coming out. Bear left the tunnel room and got out of the spider hole. The LT marked on his map the location so he could tell the demo engineers where it was located, so they could blow up the complex.

The platoon regrouped, and they continued around the LZ. They came to a small clearing completely filled with B - 52 bomb craters. Damn, Bear thought, how could anyone survive this destruction?

When the platoon was half way across the clearing, the VC opened fire on them.

They all hit the deck in a bomb crater and returned fire. The LT called in the Cobra gunships to make a run at the area. He popped smoke and the Cobras identified, As soon as the Cobras finished, the platoon moved forward toward the trees, firing their weapons. "Recon by fire" is what it was called.

As they got to the edge of the tree line, a single round was fired at them. They all hit the deck and searched the trees for the gook. Bear heard one of the "newbees" holler at him.

"Sarge," he said, "What is this?" He held up a bush limb that was covered with tiny pieces of what used to be a human being.

"That's Charlie around us."

"Where ? Where ?" yelled the newbee. He had not got Bear's meaning.

"Relax," Bear said, "That's a piece of dead VC."

The "newbee" immediately dropped the limb and began to vomit. Bear couldn't blame him. Bear had done the same thing when he had first encountered tiny human pieces lying around.

Someone hollered, "There he goes!" and the firing commenced again, but the VC disappeared into the jungle. Bear's squad followed a blood trail to another tunnel complex.

They searched the area and found three more entrances. His squad covered all the entrances and tossed in a couple of grenades at each entrance. after the noise and smoke and dust cleared, they heard a gook hollering, "Chieu Hoi," (which meant he wanted to surrender). Bear called out to him to "La Dai", which meant to come out.

Two VC came out with their hands up. Bear tied their hands, and called the LT to call for a "slick" to come and pick up the prisoners. Meanwhile, Runt donned his earplugs, flashlight, and pistol and descended into the tunnel to search it out. He brought up a Chi - com rifle, (a long Chinese communist rifle, somewhat like a 30.06 rifle), 2 AK – 47's, ammo, rice, papers, and maps. They sent all that out with the prisoners on the "slick" chopper. The LT marked the location on his map for the demo team.

They continued to sweep the area and found many more tunnels and bunker complexes.

The platoon found about a dozen more VC bodies and a lot of equipment and weapons.

By the time the demolition team showed up, the platoon had finished sweeping the whole LZ area. They pulled security around the area while the engineers did their job. It was almost dark when the platoon was extracted and flown back to Cu Chi. When they got back to Cu Chi, Bear received a telegram from the Red Cross that his son had been born a week earlier. They had a beer bash and celebrated his birth. It felt good to have a successful day like that, topped off by good news from home.

Bear had a son and he didn't even know his name. Bear hadn't held him. He didn't even know Bear existed. Please God, Bear thought, let me make it home.

LIEUTENANT CHU

On some missions in Nam, South Vietnamese Army Officers would accompany an American unit on their mission. The officers would serve as interpreters and guides as well as participating in the mission.

On the mission this particular day, the third platoon met and got to know Lieutenant Chu. He was a small man in build, but a person could tell right away that Lieutenant Chu was a leader. He was a soldier all the way through. Lieutenant Chu was all business, and he perceived that his business was to eliminate the VC and NVA enemy. Taking prisoners went against Lieutenant Chu's grain. Taking prisoners was a last resort and then only when he was given a direct order by an officer of higher authority. He hated the VC with all of his being. His family had been murdered by the VC years earlier simply because Lieutenant Chu was an officer of the South Vietnamese Army.

The area where the mission was located was the river and canal area around the South Vam Co Dong River, South of Cu

174

Chi. Bear was the scout squad leader on this particular day, and Lieutenant Chu was assigned to his squad. They were assigned to the first chopper of the three chopper sortie. The platoon had artillery support if they needed it. They had Cobra gunships to escort them on their mission. The Cobras would escort the slicks into the LZ and then stand by in case they were needed by flying around the area. The mission was to link up with a LRRP squad and sweep and search the area for the enemy.

The LRRP team had spotted many enemy bunkers and they had clashed with "Charlie" every time they had turned around. Their job was to recon, but several times they had to fight and run to protect themselves. Their "Kit Carson" scout had been killed. They had sustained some wounds. The LRRP team leader was Sgt. Buck, and he was as wild as they come. He never gave the enemy any kind of chance, and his idea of reconnaissance was to kill a few of the gooks and see what would happen. But even with all that in mind, Bear would have trusted Buck with his life more than anyone else he had met in Nam.

As usual, the scout squad was understrength, so Bear carried his own PRC - 25 (back pack radio). He had nine other men plus Lieutenant Chu in his squad. Three of the squad members were green as a gourd, and Bear hadn't yet learned their correct names. Bear wore the Sergeant E 5 insignia, but he was "acting jack". That meant that he did the job of a Sergeant E - 5, but he didn't get paid for it. By this time, Bear believed the Army had forgotten that he was just an "acting jack".

The choppers took off from the heli-pad at Cu Chi in a cloud of dust, and it took Bear a while to get the dust out of his eyes and mouth. The LRRP team had secured the LZ for the platoon so the dismount from the choppers would be fairly protected. Besides they had a Cobra gunship escort just in case "Charlie" had a surprise for them. Over the radio Bear heard the "chopper jocks" identify the color of smoke the LRRP team had popped on the LZ. Bear directed his men to prepare to dismount. He passed along to the team that the LZ would still be a cold LZ. Bear didn't want anyone to fire as they dismounted and alert "Charlie" or take a chance of hitting a LRRP team member. The chopper banked and headed in to the LZ. As Bear dismounted, Buck waved at him to come over.

"Hey! Bear! What's happenin' man ?"

"Just trying to stay alive. What do we have here?"

"Well, we got your typical bunkers along the river and canal banks to search and destroy, and some of them may be occupied," Buck chuckled as he finished his sentence. "Is that greenhorn LT with you today?"

"No, he rotated to another unit. Sergeant Brown is in charge."

"Well, hell, that's great!" exclaimed Buck. "We might get something done today."

A sickening, foul smell found its way to Bear's nostrils while they waited for Sergeant Brown to link up with them. "What is that smell?" Bear asked.

"That is or was our Kit Carson scout, Ty. He's been dead for a couple of days, but I promised him before he died that I would not leave his body in the bush. You know how these gooks are about getting to heaven in one piece. Ty did not want to be left for ol'

"Charlie" to mutilate. Those choppers left in such a hurry, I couldn't get Ty's body loaded aboard."

"31, this is 34, over," came Sergeant Brown's voice over the radio.

"This is 31, go ahead, 34," Bear replied.

"Bear where are you all?"

"Look toward the river. I'll wave my scarf." Bear took his yellow scarf off and waved it back and forth over his head until Sgt. Brown had seen it.

Sgt. Brown spotted Bear's scarf. He contacted and gathered up the other leaders, and they all proceeded toward Bear's position. Sgt. Brown moved toward Bear and Buck through the small underbrush with his RTO and two squad leaders. As soon as they got to them, they held a short meeting with Buck. Buck showed the leaders on his map where the bunkers were located. They would have to cross the river around the bend to the South to get to one of the complexes.

Bear's squad would take the lead with the LRRP team. Sgt. Brown and the second squad would be second. The third squad would bring up the rear. If anything were to happen to split up the platoon, the rendezvous point would be the LZ they just landed on. That same LZ would be where they would be picked up, also.

"Any questions?" Buck asked.

"Yeah, how do you get so lucky to get these cushy assignments?" Asked Sgt. Brown, as he laughed. Everyone chuckled.

"I don't think the ol' C.O. likes me," Buck answered. Even Lt. Chu chuckled. The leaders all went back to their squads and had a short meeting.

"Okay, you all listen up," Bear said. "We are the lead squad. The LRRPs will take point. We'll walk in single file but keep spread out. Let's be quiet and no smoking. Buck tells me there are gooks everywhere. We have three bunker complexes to check out. After we have checked all three, we will blow what we can with the C - 4 we have. We are looking for anything of value. The C.O. would like to have some prisoners if possible."

Lt. Chu grunted at the last statement and Bear knew Chu didn't like the prisoner bit. "What's wrong Chu?" Bear asked.

"Cock - a - dow VC," (meaning to kill VC) Chu answered.

"Now listen, Chu," Bear said, "you follow orders, understand?"

Lt. Chu didn't answer but his glare told Bear to go to hell. "Let's move out." Bear said. They started down the river bank out of sight of the other side and well off any trails that might be booby - trapped. The first bunker complex was about a half click. The complex was made up of three bunkers in a triangle position. The bunkers were empty, but the platoon moved in cautiously.

"Bear, take your men and check out the bunkers," Sgt. Brown said. "Second and third squads, set up a perimeter around the area."

"Okay, men. Let's split up in groups of three. Each group take a bunker," Bear said. Bear looked at two of the greenhorns and Lt. Chu and said, "You three come with me."

"Mind if we get in the game?" asked Buck.

"It's up to you all."

"You four go by twos with those groups, and I'll go with Bear," Buck instructed.

They approached the bunkers slowly. This was not the time to get reckless. Buck grabbed one of the greenhorns and said, "Stop! Don't move a muscle. Bear, there's a booby - trap here!"

Bear moved over to the two and sure enough, there was a trip - wire hooked up to a "bouncing Betty". A "bouncing Betty" would explode about waist high. A person couldn't get away from the blast.

"Well, we're in luck!" Bear said. "Bud you stopped just in time. Now, move your right foot back slowly." After the greenhorn had moved back, Bear and Buck disarmed the booby trap.

"Whew! Bear, that was close!" Buck sighed.

"Yeah, I know. Let's me and you check this out, Buck. You two stay right here," Bear said to the greenhorns.

Buck and Bear moved in and checked out the bunker. It hadn't been occupied for a while. There were no hidden doors or spider holes. They regrouped and got the same report from the others. The only booby trap was the one that had already been found. Some joker had left it behind for an unsuspecting soul.

Buck said, "Okay, from here we need to move to the bend in the river. About half way around the bend, there is a canal that goes back to the north. There are bunkers on either side of the canal. It looks like an unloading point for sampans (boats) from the river. At the end of the canal is the point where our Kit Carson scout met his maker."

"Mount up! Sgt." Brown whispered. "Single file same-o same-o." The command was passed on down through the ranks.

The sun was high in the sky and the humidity was sucking the life out of all their bodies. Bear could never believe how wringing wet he could be on the outside, and still have cotton-mouth because he was so dry on the inside.

The platoon had about a half click to move to their next point. The heat and humidity slowed them down considerably and the bush wasn't helping much either. The bush was thick with underbrush. It had been decided to cut across country to the far bend of the canal, split into two groups and search each side at the same time. Bear's squad with Lt. Chu and the LRRP team would take the near side, while the second and third squads with Sgt. Brown would take the far side.

They were almost to their destination when the point man motioned for them to stop and get down. They all froze and waited. Bear could hear gooks talking in the not too far distance. Bear dropped his ruck sack and radio and crawled up with Buck to the point. Bear's heart was pounding so hard in his ears, he could have sworn it was a bass drum and everyone in the world could hear it. Buck and Bear finally reached the point man.

"What's up, Jake?" Buck asked.

"Two, maybe three gooks over there by the bunker by the small boat," said the point man.

"Well, one good thing is that they have their backs to us. Jake, you and I will circle around until we are facing them and find out how many there are. Bear, we will hand signal you, and you all can move into position behind the bunker on this side. Let's give them a chance to surrender first. Maybe we can make the C.O. happy."

"Right on, Buck," Bear said, as Jake and Buck moved out.

Bear crawled back to Sergeant Brown and told him the plan. Brown immediately set up a perimeter for their own protection. Then Bear, Brown, the other three LRRPs and Lt. Chu moved into a position several meters behind the bunker and waited. It seemed like a long time until Buck and Jake got into position, but it was really only a few minutes. Just as Buck started to signal Bear, one of the gooks came around the bunker toward Bear to take a leak.

They all held their breath. The gook would have had a heart attack if only he knew the enemy was so close. He was unarmed. As the gook walked back to the front of the bunker, Buck signaled for Bear to move in closer. Bear's group moved right up to the bunker. The canal was only about fifteen feet wide so Jake and Buck were fairly close, too. The gooks had been fishing and were eating.

Sergeant Brown told Lt. Chu to tell the gooks to "chuehoi" (surrender) and that they were surrounded. Lt. Chu hollered out in Vietnamese as the group came around both sides of the bunker and Jake and Buck showed themselves on the other side. The group caught them totally by surprise with their chopsticks and cups in their hands and their rifles too far away to get to. The VC immediately put their hands on their heads and surrendered. As Bear's group tied their hands behind their backs, Jake and Buck kept them covered from the other side.

Lt. Chu started interrogating one of them in Vietnamese. In a blink of an eye, he kicked one of the VC prisoners. He put his hand over the prisoners mouth and stabbed the VC with his knife. The other two prisoners' eyes got as big as saucers. The gook died without a sound as the blood gushed from his back.

"Damn it all, Chu," Sergeant Brown yelled, "What the hell are you doing? Get away from here. We're taking these prisoners back."

"Kill VC!" Lt. Chu snapped back.

Bear jumped to Lt. Chu and pushed him back out of the way. "Listen, Chu, we're taking these two back. Now, you got that?" Bear shouted as they stared at each other. Finally, Lt. Chu backed off and sat down.

Buck sent Jake back to fetch the troops. They checked out the bunker and the gooks' weapons and gear.

Bear had mixed feelings about Chu killing the VC. Bear knew he was the enemy, but he also knew that the VC was unarmed and bound. As far as Bear was concerned, that was real cold. It was murder.

The platoon and the LRRPs divided up into the same groups as Sgt. Brown had instructed earlier. The two prisoners stayed with Bear as they searched the other bunkers. Sgt. Brown sank the boat with his entrenching tool by knocking holes in the bottom. The rest of the bunkers were empty, but they had been occupied very recently. In fact, there were sandal prints everywhere. This was an unloading area for sure.

Bear reached the river's edge just in time to see a sampan trying to maneuver into the canal area at the bend across the river where Bear was headed next. Bear grabbed one of the greenhorn's grenade launcher and fired. He hit the sampan, and some VC jumped off and ran, while the rest of the group fired. Bear fired the M 79 grenade launcher again and the sampan exploded in a million pieces and sank. It must have been loaded with explosives. They waited. Over his radio Bear could hear Sgt.

Brown talking to the C.O. about what had happened and was asking for instructions. The radio was silent while the C.O. contemplated the next move.

"Bear, what's up?" Buck asked.

"The old man is thinking things over. I hope we don't have to swim that nasty river."

"What's a matter, Bear? You <u>do</u> need a bath."

After firing on the enemy over on the other side and probably alerting every gook in the countryside that they were here, Bear didn't fancy swimming across that wide river, like a sitting duck.

"Blue Tiger 34, this is Blue Tiger 6, over," came the C.O. over the radio.

"This is Blue Tiger 34, over," said Sgt. Brown.

"Sarge, send a group over to check that bunker complex across the river. Give us the coordinates on the three complexes, and we will call in an artillery barrage after you get out of the area."

Sgt. Brown gave the coordinates of the bunkers to the C.O. over the radio. "Bear," said Sgt. Brown. "You take Lt. Chu and the LRRP team and go check out the other side of the river. The rest of us will wire up what C - 4 we have to blow as many of these bunkers as we can."

Bear hated this part. Someone would have to swim across the river with a rope wrapped around his shoulders, so that he could tie the rope to a tree on the other side. Bear figured that someone would be him. They had brought a rope for just that use. Once the rope was in place, the weapons and ammo and radio would be ferried across on inflated air mattresses.

Bear swam about half - way across the river when "Charlie" opened up on him. Bear was a sitting duck and he hated that feeling of not being in control. He dove under the water as bullets hit around him. He stayed under the water as long as he could, while he swam toward his destination. When Bear came up for air, the VC fired at him again. He dove under the water again and swam as long as he could, until he was nearly out of breath. As he broke the surface, he could hear the battle raging. Bullets bounced around him again so he dove deep once again. Bear's lungs were about to explode. He couldn't do this much longer. If he did not reach the far bank this time, "Charlie" would probably kill him.

Bear felt the bank of the river when he came up for air. The firing had stopped. The VC had turned tail and run. Bear filled his lungs with air. What a great feeling! He tied the rope to a tree and waved to the others on the other bank. They pulled the rope tight and tied it to a tree on their side of the river. The weapons, ammo, and radio were ferried across by the rope. They had one hand on the rope and one on the air mattresses and kicked their legs and scooted across the river toward Bear.

The rest of the squad crossed the river without any more trouble— unless you count a few leeches as trouble. They mounted up and continued toward the bunker complex. After a while, they came across a blood trail.

"Probably one of those gooks from the sampan," Buck said. "Let's follow it a ways."

They followed the blood trail through the bush for about fifty meters until they came to another trail. "I bet this trail goes to the bunker complex," Buck whispered.

"Yeah, I just hope there ain't a whole company up there," Bear said.

They followed the trail of blood until they finally got to the bunker area.

"Okay," Buck said, "let's spread out and check out those bunkers."

The group broke off into pairs and began to check the bunkers out. Bear took Lt. Chu with him. They followed the blood trail down towards the bunkers. Soon the blood trail ended at one of the entrances. Chu and Bear circled the bunker. There was no sign of life. Bear entered the bunker first. The blood trail stopped in the center of the bunker. His heart was pounding at this point, and his adrenalin was going crazy. If someone had said "Boo!", Bear would have jumped over the moon.

"Spider hole," Chu whispered. Bear nodded in agreement. They searched around and found an edge to the lid. Chu motioned that he would raise it up, and Bear would fire. Chu grasped the edge and flung open the trap door. Bear saw the figure of a man and pulled the trigger. Click. Nothing! Bear almost died of fright.

His M - 16 misfired. He ejected the misfire and rammed home another shell.

By this time, Chu had waved Bear off. The gook was already dead. He had bled to death. The feeling of fear Bear felt at that moment had him shaking so badly he could hardly hold still. Chu sensed that fear as he nodded for Bear to leave. They finished checking out the bunkers and found nothing else. They regrouped and went back to where the watery bridge was located. They repeated the process in reverse as they swam back across the river and pulled their gear on the mattresses. Buck was the last to swim back across. He untied the rope and wrapped it across his shoulders and swam back across.

Sergeant Brown had all the C - 4 charges ready to set off as soon as they got back.

"All right you guys," Sgt. Brown said, "be alert." As soon as we blow the charges, we will have every gook in the area on our tail, if we haven't already.

The charges were set off by the last squad to leave as they moved out toward the LZ. The sound was deafening when the charges went off. As they left for the LZ, Sergeant Brown radioed the C.O., so that the choppers would be at the LZ soon. The platoon and the LRRPs moved back to the LZ a lot faster than they came.

Bear reached the edge of the LZ first and observed the area for a while before moving into position to secure it. Bear's squad and the LRRP team were going to secure the far side. As they reached the middle of the LZ, they stopped to set up the command post.

Bear, Sgt. Brown, Lt Chu and the two prisoners were going to stay in the middle of the LZ at the CP.

"Something doesn't feel right," Buck said.

"I know," Bear replied. "I have a bad feeling, too."

"Bear, do you see Ty's Body? asked Buck.

"No, by golly, I don't."

At that moment, the far edge of the LZ came alive with the sounds of AK – 47's. They hit the ground and returned fire.

"They got Ty's body," said Buck. "They will mess him up for sure. Bear let me have your radio."

Bear crawled over to Buck. They studied the map and called "arty". As Buck called off the coordinates over the radio, Bear double - checked his map for the coordinates.

"Damn, Buck, those are the coordinates of our position."

"I know, but we don't have time for an adjustment. Besides, "arty" is always long on the first rounds anyway." Buck shouted, "Keep your heads down! Here comes the "arty"".

In a matter of seconds, the rounds came whistling overhead and exploded in the far woodline. Dirt, clods, pieces of wood, metal and who knows what else, sprayed all over the group from the sky. Bear could hear the gooks screaming between rounds. The artillery fire stopped after what seemed like a dozen rounds being fired. As soon as the explosions ceased, Buck ordered his men to secure the far woodline. The group fired and maneuvered to the woodline. They received no return fire. The enemy was gone.

Buck waved to Bear from the woodline to let him know his side of the LZ was secure.

Bear caught Lt. Chu giving the two VC prisoners the evil eye. Bear cautioned Chu again to leave them alone. Lt. Chu had "kill the VC" written all over his face. In about fifteen minutes the choppers arrived with a Cobra gunship escort. Bear popped smoke. The "slicks" identified the color of the smoke and flew into the LZ to pick them up. The Cobra gunships skirted the area for protection, while the grunts loaded the "slicks". Bear's squad, Lt. Chu, the LRRP team, and the two VC prisoners mounted the first chopper. They all mounted the choppers with no problem. Although Bear's chopper was really crowded.

As soon as the choppers cleared the area, Sgt. Brown called on the radio for artillery to pound the three bunker complex areas. They were flying back to base camp when Lt. Chu started interrogating the two VC prisoners. He had to get real close because of the chopper and wind noise. Bear realized too late that he should have separated Lt. Chu and the prisoners and put the prisoners in the middle of the chopper. Lt. Chu and the VC argued. Lt. Chu became more irate by the second. The choppers were several hundred feet above the ground by this time. Lt. Chu got in the face of one VC and shouted. Lt. Chu surprised everyone when he pushed the gook out of the chopper doorway. Bear looked out of the doorway in time to see the gook hit the ground.

Bear separated Chu and the last VC.

The remaining gook began talking ninety miles an hour. Bear couldn't believe what he had just witnessed. Lt. Chu cold bloodedly killed that gook and didn't show any sign of remorse. Lt. Chu was cold hearted.

The radio transmission shocked Bear back to reality. "Blue Tiger 31, this is 34, over," said Sgt. Brown over the radio.

"This is 34, go ahead Sarge," Bear answered.

"What was that falling out of your chopper?" Sgt. Brown asked.

"Well Sarge, you know those Victor Charlie's we had? Well, we just have one now." The radio was silent. The silence was deafening.

Even after all these years later, Lt. Chu is still the coldest man Bear ever met.

Hate will make you that way.

V C SURPRISE

Many days were spent on sweeps and search and destroy missions. Just as many nights were spent on ambush patrols. There were many enemy contacts during this time, but not any major engagements until one day without warning a simple search and destroy mission turned into a battle in which Bear and the third platoon had to fight their way out of a hot PZ.

About 1300 a LRRP team was extracted from a hot PZ. The scramble horn went off and the third platoon ran to the waiting choppers to be air lifted to and inserted in the same area where the LRRP team had just left shooting their way out. Red Horse 6, the 3/17 squadron commander, was flying over the area in his helicopter and decided that a force needed to go in to check out the VC bunker complex and see what size a VC force was in the area.

Bear sat and watched the other members of his squad and listened to the slap of chopper blades. Bear silently went through his ritual he repeated in a situation like this which was to think the

Lord's Prayer and Psalm 23. Bear wondered what was on the other soldier's minds. The third platoon had only twenty one men today which left Bear's scout squad with six men counting himself. Bear carried his own radio today so as to free up the other scouts. As the choppers approached the LZ the door gunner opened fire. Bear and his squad stepped out on the skid anticipating the helicopter pilot cutting the engines back. In that instant the squad would jump off the skids onto the ground and set up a perimeter. Waiting too long to jump would mean a high jump from the chopper to the ground because the chopper never really landed. The pilot would cut the power when close to the ground and then open up the engine to full power to fly out. In that instant the soldiers had better be off the chopper or else it was a long way to the ground. The pilots were sitting ducks in their plexi - glass canopies in the front of the Huey chopper; therefore, they didn't like being on the ground very long. And who could blame them.

As soon as the platoon was on the ground, each squad sent out a clover leaf patrol to check out the immediate area. The patrols turned up nothing so the platoon began to sweep toward the Northeast where the bunker complex was located. Bear and his squad led the way through the waist high elephant grass. The day was hot and humid and the heat intensified in the tall grass.

As the platoon neared the bunker complex, the platoon sergeant gave the command to recon by five to try and draw out any VC if there were any in the area. The only bad thing about recon by five was that the VC would know your position and that you were in the area. This day the VC force would follow the third platoon at a safe distance waiting for the right time to attack. The platoon swept through a sloppy, swampy area for about five hundred meters before reaching a canal which was about thirty feet wide. The main bunker complex was over across the canal. Bear led the way across the canal in waist deep mud with water up to his chest. It was hard work and everyone was exhausted by the time the canal was crossed.

The platoon sergeant decided to set up an L - shaped ambush in the jungle surrounding the bunker complex and rest while waiting for the VC to possibly return. The squads put out claymore mines and waited and rested.

While Bear was putting out his claymore mines, he was startled by a very large snake slithering through the bush toward the canal. The snake must have been ten feet long and four inches in diameter.

The platoon soon settled into their three man positions to wait. Most of the men were eating their "C" rations and resting when the VC surprise was sprung. Out of the quiet, several RPGs exploded all around the ambush area. Luckily no one was hit during this vulnerable time. The VC force had followed the platoon and had waited for the right moment to strike.

During the first explosion that was near Bear's position, Bear had jumped over the nearby canal dike and was in the water and muck up to his neck. He had not seen the enemy as yet as he fired across the canal. Actually, nobody knew exactly where the RPG rounds were fired from. After a short while the sound of gunfire stopped while everyone searched the area with their eyes trying to spot the enemy. By this time the dead underbrush near Bear was on fire and the smoke made the visibility near zero. Also the smoke made it hard for the soldiers downwind to breathe. Bear was one of them.

"Bear get that fire put out!" Yelled the platoon sergeant.

Bear eased up out of the canal only to come face to face with the big snake he had seen earlier. The snake was wrapped around the small trees that lined the canal and was probably disturbed by the fire too. Bear wanted to kill the snake because he felt that the only good snake was a dead snake, but the fire and smoke were a more important problem right now. But if the snake moved he was a dead snake. Bear crawled up over the canal berm toward the fire. He unloaded the radio and crawled about twenty meters to the fire.

He took off his wet shirt and while lying on his back begun to beat the flames out with his shirt. His eyes burned with the smoke. Bear could hardly breathe as he continued to beat the fire out. Finally the fire was put out and the smoke gradually went away. Bear was burned a little on his hands and back. Bear crawled back to the canal berm where he had left his rifle and radio.

"Blue Tiger this is Wild Horse, over."

"This is Blue Tiger go ahead Wild Horse." Bear answered.

"We are near your position, pop smoke."

"Roger, Wild Horse. Popping smoke."

Bear threw a smoke grenade and the Cobra gun ship pilot identified the color of smoke.

"Blue Tiger, where do you want our rounds, over."

"Wild Horse, unload East of the smoke, over."

"Roger, Blue Tiger."

The gunships made several gun runs over the area. In the meantime, the VC had moved around behind Bear's position. The medic, Doc, had crawled over to Bear's position to check his burns. Bear and Doc spotted some VC moving toward them. Bear took Doc's M - 79 and fired several M - 79 rounds at them killing one about fifty meters away. The fire fight continued all around the platoon area as the VC soldiers had surrounded the area. Bear fired ten more rounds of the M - 79 grenades. Doc killed one VC with Bear's M - 16 as he appeared across the canal area. Two VC appeared out of the jungle to Bear's left. Bear fired several grenades at them and blew them out of sight.

"Bear, get your unspent claymores in and get your squad together. We're pulling out to the PZ." the platoon sergeant called on the radio.

"Roger that, Sarge." Bear passed along the message.

The platoon firing constantly moved back across the canal toward the closest open area to be picked up by the choppers. More Cobra gunships showed up and covered the platoon movement to the PZ.

When the slicks showed up, there were only two of them. Bear's scout squad would have to wait until another chopper showed up. The platoon was being air lifted to a nearby air boat unit support base close by on the river so the wait wouldn't be long. The platoon popped smoke and the slicks identified the color. The door gunners came in firing their machine guns as the gunships circled the area firing their rockets and guns. The first two choppers loaded the troops without any trouble. The choppers came in from East to West in a hurry.

The gunships kept circling the area as Bear's squad huddled in the tall elephant grass watching and waiting. The sound of a whistle broke the silence. The VC used whistles to direct their soldiers and rally them. The grass was so tall Bear couldn't see them, but he could hear voices. Bear hoped that the gunships would keep them at bay while they waited for the chopper to return.

"Blue Tiger this is Bandit 6 over."

"Bandit 6 this is Blue Tiger, over."

"Blue Tiger we are coming in West to East this time. What is your location,"

"Bandit 6 we are popping smoke. Identify. Be advised that Victor Charlie is in the area. We can hear their voices, but we can't see them."

Roger that Blue Tiger. Keep you heads down. We'll come in firing."

Bear could hear that sweet sound of the blades slapping the air. The chopper came in with the door gunners blazing away at the woodlines. As soon as the chopper touched down, Bear and his men scrambled inside with bullets bouncing everywhere. In an instant the chopper was up and away. Bear peered down out of the chopper and saw many VC run out of the woodline firing up at the chopper. Bear quickly jerked his head back inside. As soon as they left the area, some F – 100's made a bomb run on the PZ. The platoon made it out another time by the skin of their teeth.

Bear took a quick check of his men. Everyone was okay but wringing wet with sweat and very tired. It was then Bear noticed that his pants were ripped almost off him and he had a couple of leeches on his thigh sucking away. Bear squirted mosquito repellent on them to make them fall off. It stung but he got them off and threw them out of the chopper.

Tomorrow one of the platoons would go back in with a demolition team to blow up the bunker complex. The VC bodies would probably be gone as usual. Bear had lost down to 180 pounds by now. He weighed 210 pounds when he left the U.S. almost a year ago.

Bear was getting close to going home on the freedom bird. But right now Bear was too pooped to pop, so he closed his eyes for a short nap. And dreamed of home.

NIGHT AMBUSH - KILL TEAMS

The reaction missions became coupled with night ambush patrols. Bear was close to going home - he was what was called a "short timer". The months and days Bear had been counting were now down to a few days and hours. Bear tried to keep his focus on his job so that he wouldn't make some stupid mistake. Stupid mistakes could cost you your life.

The troop was going on a mission as a whole search and destroy unit. Bear's platoon would be left in the area to set up a night ambush when the other two platoons were picked up. That way the VC were tricked into thinking the American soldiers were all gone. Sometimes two platoons would go out on a mission and one platoon would be left for a night ambush. And a few times a platoon would go out on a mission and only one squad would be left behind. The order had come down from higher command that they wanted body counts; therefore, kill teams were created to gauge a successful night ambush. The kill team's job after the ambush was to crawl out in the night and retrieve dead bodies and their weapons. The VC would drag off their dead after a fight and that made the mission seem unsuccessful. Also the VC wanted to bury their dead and retrieve their own weapons and ammo. That practice by the VC played mind games on the Americans because if there were no bodies how could the grunts know how many they killed in a fight. So kill teams would risk their lives and sometimes have to finish off the wounded VC to save themselves. It was a hairy job at best and most guys didn't care for it at all. But when higher ups said they wanted bodies then by golly there was going to be bodies. After all, the grunts were at the bottom of the chain of command and that meant they did what they were told. When this all started, Bear wondered if he could kill his enemy that way. But when his time came he did what he had to do to survive like all good soldiers.

The LRRPs had found many bunker complexes and trails in the area of that day's operation. They had also witnessed a VC regiment movement in the area. The LRRPs were extracted from the area of operation the evening before. B - 52 bombers bombed the area that night. In base camp D Troop could hear and feel the bomb blasts. The whole troop wondered if that was where they would be the next day. Bear was in the lead chopper with his scout squad and he saw the bomb craters all over the area of operation. Yes, the bombers were bombing that area last night. Bear thought to himself as the choppers descended to the LZ - How could anyone be alive in that devastation? Bear and his squad jumped from the chopper and ran to the woodline to set up security for the rest of the troop. The first sortie of choppers transported all the troop's scout squads to secure the LZ. There was no firing of weapons just the unforgettable but sweet sound of the choppers. Bear watched into the bush waiting for all hell to break loose but nothing happened. After the whole troop dismounted, the platoon leaders assembled their platoons and organized them for the search and destroy mission. The troops had plenty of grenades and C - 4 explosives to blowup any bunkers and tunnels.

Mouse was the tunnel rat in the third platoon. He was a small man just the right size to crawl in the tunnels and check them out. Thus he was nicknamed Mouse. Mouse carried a .22 automatic pistol. He would put earplugs in his ears and with his pistol and flashlight he would be lowered into the tunnel. Before the tunnel rats would go into the tunnels grenades would be thrown in the entrance to insure there was no immediate danger to the tunnel rat. If many entrances and air holes or spider holes were suspected, smoke grenades and /or CS gas grenades were thrown in the tunnels first. That way the smoke and/or gas would show where the other holes were located. Then after the air cleared the tunnel rats would go in and check them out. Bear popped a smoke grenade and threw it in a tunnel entrance. The platoon watched and waited. Smoke came out a little distance from the entrance. His squad checked out the other end and waited for the smoke to clear. All around them bunkers were being blown-up. It was very noisy and Bear jumped every time an explosion went off.

"Getting kind of jumpy aren't you Bear?" Mouse asked with a grin.

"Yep, I am getting too short for this crap."

The tunnel went straight down and to the right toward the other entrance. Mouse tied a rope around both his ankles to be lowered into the tunnel head first.

"Okay, Mouse you ready?" Bear asked.

Some of the other men started to help Mouse into the hole. but Mouse spoke up as usual.

"No! No! I want Bear to lower me in the tunnel. Bear if anything happens don't leave me down there. You pull my butt out of there fast."

Bear replied. "You bet, now in you go."

Bear lowered Mouse a little ways into the tunnel just enough so Mouse could use his flashlight to look down the long dark tunnel. Then Mouse went all the way inside. Bear kept lowering the rope as Mouse moved along inside the tunnel. After a while Mouse appeared at the other end.

"Nothing down there but tunnel."

It must have been used for hiding personnel inside. Bear let go of the rope and Mouse pulled it to the other end. As Bear leaned back on his left arm to get up he felt something metallic. It was a Coke can half buried in the ground.

"Damn!" Bear said.

"What's wrong Bear" someone asked.

"I think I'm on a booby - trap"

Everyone quickly backed away from Bear.

The platoon sergeant came up to Bear's position about that same time.

"What's going on here."

"I think I'm on a booby - trap.", Sarge. Bear answered.

"Okay, don't panic. The rest of you move way back out of here."

The platoon sergeant got on his knees and got out his bayonet and probed around the Coke can. He peered in the small opening.

"Well, Bear. I believe you got a Coke can here filled with metal pieces and probably booby - trapped. Do you have any pressure on the can now?

"Yes" Bear replied as the sweat ran into his eyes.

"Okay, the bomb probably has a pressure release trigger. Now let me have your rifle. As soon as we are all clear, I want you to roll as fast as you can away from the area. It is <u>real</u> important Bear that you move as quickly as you can."

As soon as the platoon sergeant moved back with the others, they all got down on the ground as low as they could get.

Bear took a deep breath. He was trembling, but he knew he had to settle down. He had one chance. And that was too pull away and roll as fast as he could roll.

In an instant Bear rolled away and the booby - trap went off. The explosion deafened Bear for a while but he was okay. Everyone took a deep breath and ran over to see if Bear was Okay.

"I'm okay. I'm too damn short for this stuff."

"He's okay. Let's get back to our business. Blow this tunnel. Let's go. Move it." Sarge said.

"Thanks, Sarge." Bear said.

"Don't mention it, Bear. We've got to get you home in one piece."

"Amen to that." Bear replied. Most of the hot, humid day was spent destroying the VC complex. About mid afternoon the slicks came in to get the rest of the troop. The third platoon hid in the jungle as the others were air lifted out. The platoon set up an ambush on the main trail coming in to the bunker complex. The main trail branched off into two trails like a Y.

The platoon set up in a triangle - shaped ambush between the two trails and waited for any VC that might come down the trail during the night. Each position contained three men. each soldier would take his turn at watch during the night. Usually it was a two hour rotating watch with each man on watch twice. The other two men would rest if they could. The platoon set out their claymore mines along the edge of the trails and made fighting holes where they could. After eating what rations they had, night began to fall. In the bush, the night was darker than dark, and it came early and stayed late.

The first three watches came and went without any trouble except for all the bugs and mosquitos. Bear started the fourth watch, his second watch of the night, when he heard voices. He woke up the others in his position which was on the right fork. The voices seemed to be coming from the left fork not too far away. Everyone was awake anxiously waiting. At first two gooks came down the trail jabbering away. When they got to the main trail, they called back to the others following them. Bear's breathing became light and his pulse rate raced. His heart pounded in his throat. His mouth was dry. The smell of death closed in as the main body of VC appeared on the trail. Bear was on the trail away from the VC, but he could make out shadows in the night. Bear could hardly contain himself. The two VC out front started down the trail Bear was on. So that's why we haven't sprung the ambush Bear thought to himself. The ambush was waiting to see the size of the force and where they were headed. The platoon sergeant had given orders to hold out fire until he blew his claymore first. The platoon waited until the whole VC force was in the kill zone. The platoon sergeant blew his claymore, and when he did twenty more claymores went off around the triangle. The VC were yelling and moaning as they were blown to pieces by the mines. One VC ran through to the inside of the perimeter

213

and ran a circle and back out before he was shot down. The tracers lit up the jungle as the soldiers emptied their weapons into the VC group. The VC never fired a shot back. They were totally wiped out in a matter of minutes. Some probably escaped but Bear didn't think so.

The firing stopped. The platoon sergeant yelled out to get the weapons and bodies off the trail. Each position sent out a man for the kill team. Bear crawled out toward the VC bodies in front of him. He heard moaning and then, he heard single shots ring out in the night air. The first two VC Bear came to were dead. He stripped them of their web gear and weapons and drug them back inside the perimeter one at a time. Bear then picked up all the weapons and web gear and brought them back inside. There were twenty dead VC bodies inside the perimeter by morning. The platoon captured one rocket launcher, ten AK - 47 rifles, and two pistols plus all the web gear and ammo.

When the sun came up, the platoon policed up everything after searching the bodies and hiked towards the LZ to be picked up. They left the bodies side by side to rot in the jungle. The pickup was without incident. The platoon flew back to base camp successful in their mission but lost in their thoughts.

Short - timer Bear left base camp that very afternoon to get ready to go home on the freedom bird. It took a few days of processing, then he flew on home. Bear finally made it home alive, but at least ten years older.

EPILOGUE

In part, I attribute my Viet Nam survival to my high school coaches and my Army drill instructors who instilled in me from day one to never ever give up no matter what happens.

The Viet Nam War to me was very frustrating to say the least. The VC took a page out of our own history books concerning guerrilla warfare. In our own American Revolution we fought the British in much the same way. Hit hard and run. Many times we never saw the enemy. To me the war was nothing like the John Wayne movies I had watched as a boy. Many times a "grunt" could not tell the good guys from the bad guys.

The war did not seem as personal when the enemy was shooting at you in a fire fight.

You shot back because it was either you or him that was to die. The unconfirmed kills didn't seem to bother me as much as the kills where I saw the haunting eyes of the dead staring at me. I had numerous nightmares about those eyes when I returned home.

I still on occasion see those eyes staring at me. They are locked in my memory, and I'll never be able to forget. I have learned to live with the memories and put them back in the hell where they belong, but I still remember.

Various days and times of the year still to this day jog my memory about Viet Nam.

Memorial day reminds me of the death of a friend, John Sinnock. My wedding anniversary on July the first reminds me of the pleading eyes of a dying boy and his father.

The fireworks at night on July the fourth reminds me of illumination rounds, trip flares, tracer bullets, LP, and ambush patrols. Veterans Day reminds me of all my buddies from Viet Nam. Some of whom I have never seen or heard from again, and I feel like a small part of me has died. The playing of taps reminds me of our dead and wounded and the ceremonies we never had for some of them. At times when the wind blows, I think I can still here helicopter blades slapping the air. The rain reminds me of the rainy season and the question — Will it ever stop raining? For me,

Ben, after all these years the rain has finally stopped. Forget! How could anyone ever forget?

Thou shalt not kill. I have asked God for forgiveness, and I still ask God to forgive me from time to time. The Bible makes it clear in Hebrews 9:27 that "it is appointed for men to die once", but I believe that warriors die many deaths.

GLOSSARY OF TERMS

AMBUSH - To surprise attack your enemy from hidden positions.

ARVN - South Vietnamese Army Soldier.

BANDOLEER TORPEDO - A long slender explosive device that can be pushed through the perimeter wire to blow a hole in the wire to get into that camp.

BEEHIVE ROUNDS - Artillery rounds that are filled with millions of small nail – like devices used in close quarter combat.

BOOBY TRAP - Various types of traps set by the enemy - explosive and non-explosive – to kill or wound people.

BOUNCING BETTY - A type of booby trap bomb that when tripped by a trip wire would bounce up about waist high before exploding.

BUSH / BOONIES - Jungle or countryside

CHARLIE - Enemy soldier.

CHIEU HOI - Surrender or open arms

CHOPPER - Helicopter

CLICK - 1,000 meters

CO - Commanding Officer

COBRA GUNSHIPS - A helicopter - The Huey Cobra - with advanced weapons systems, slim silhouette and high speed and manueverability. The two pilots sat one behind the other in the canopy. Armed with rockets, miniguns and other arsenal.

CONCERTINA WIRE - Large coiled barbed wire used to enclose a camp.

CP - Command Post

DIDI MOI - Get out of here fast.

DUSTED OFF - Dead and wounded evacuated by helicopter.

EAGLE FLIGHT MISSION - A mission where the scout choppers and gunships would fly low and fast to draw out the enemy - after which the slicks would insert the infantry to fight and / or search the area.

FIRE BASE / FIRE SUPPORT BASE - Usually a small outpost base where artillery units supported the troops in the field. It was also used as a jumping off place for various missions.

FIRE FIGHT - A term used for the actual battle or skirmish.

FREE FIRE ZONE - Usually enemy territory where soldiers were allowed to shoot before being shot at first.

GOOK - A term used for Vietnamese people.

GRUNTS - Infantry foot soldiers who fought the enemy on the ground.

GUNSHIPS - Helicopters loaded with rockets and other arsenal

HOOCH - Vietnamese hut or the simple housing in a basecamp.

HOT LZ - A landing zone under enemy fire.

HOT PZ - A pickup zone under enemy fire.

KIA - Killed in action.

LA DAI - Come here.

LP - LISTENING POST - An early warning position made up of about three soldiers with a radio placed outside the perimeter of a camp to report enemy movement.

LRRP - Long Range Reconnaissance Patrol usually consisted of five Rangers and a Vietnamese Scout (Kit Carson) put out into the bush to gather information.

LT - Lieutenant - Usually a platoon leader

LZ - Landing Zone - Open area where helicopters land or unload troops or supplies.

M - 14 RIFLE - Semi - Automatic Rifle that fired 7.62 MM caliber bullets.

M-16 RIFLE - Lighter weight semi to automatic rifle that fired .223 caliber bullets.

M- 60 MACHINE GUN - Belt fed air cooled machine gun that fired 7.62 MM caliber bullets.

M - 79 GRENADE LAUNCHER - Hand held launcher that fired several different kinds of grenades.

MIA - Missing In Action.

MOTOR POOL - Place where vehicles were kept.

MPC - Military Payment Certificate - "Funny Money" Soldiers were paid with in Viet Nam as the use of U.S. currency was a "NO -NO".

NEWBEE OR FNG - Inexperienced "Green" Soldiers just in from the states.

NO FIRE ZONE - An area where U.S. Soldiers could not fire unless fired upon.

N V A - North Vietnamese Army Soldiers.

OPCON - Temporarily attached or assigned to another unit.

PERIMETER - An area with established and secured boundaries.

PIASTERS - Vietnamese money.

P T S D - (Post Traumatic Stress Disorder) - A post Viet Nam War term synonymous with battle fatigue or shell shock as used in previous wars. The difference being that most Viet Nam War soldiers had very few positive homecoming experiences. Viet Nam veterans did their tour of duty and were thrust back into society without any time to heal from their traumatic experiences. The Viet Nam War soldiers were literally in a battle for their lives one day and back in the states the next day. Many felt abandoned and alone and tried to cope with life by pushing these traumatic experiences into the back of their mind. They never dealt with these experiences and so they never healed. These underlying problems caused a lot of veterans to turn to drugs and alcohol for inner peace, but eventually their life exploded into the Hell they thought they had left behind. Feelings of anger, frustration, sadness, guilt, and terror haunted them. Many had never cried for lost buddies. They hurt inside but didn't know why. Many marriages and relationships were ruined for no apparent reason. Thus veteran counseling centers were created to to help the Viet Nam veterans heal. Many veterans have been healed but many are still searching for peace of mind.

PUNJI STAKES - A booby trap of pointed bamboo stakes usually dipped in human waste driven into the ground sometimes in a covered hole so that when a soldier would step on them the stakes would penetrate their calf or foot.

P Z - Pickup Zone - Area where troops are to be picked up

R & R - Rest and relaxation - a vacation.

RECON MISSION - A mission used mainly for collecting information about a particular area such as enemy troop movement, strength, etc.

RENDEZVOUS POINT - A place designated ahead of time to meet.

R P G - Rocket propelled grenade

R T O - Radio Operator who carried a backpack radio (model # PRC-25) for communication purposes.

SAMPAN - A small Vietnamese boat. The VC used them to transport troops and supplies.

SLICK - Helicopters used for transporting troops and supplies (also dead and wounded) with a door gunner on each side each armed with a M-60 machinegun.

SORTIE - A group of helicopters flying in staggered formation.

SPIDER HOLE - A VC fighting hole with a covering that may lead to a tunnel complex.

STAND DOWN - Time given for rest and regrouping.

TOP - Top ranked Sergeant in a unit.

TOUR OF DUTY - Time a soldier had to spend in country before going home usually twelve to thirteen months.

V C - Viet Cong Soldier.

VULTURE FLIGHT MISSION - A mission where the slicks loaded with soldiers circled the sky high above an area being bombarded by artillery, jet fighters and gunships afterwhich the soldiers would be inserted to check out the area or fight the enemy.

W I A - Wounded In Action

X O - Executive Officer.

ADDENDUM

a. STATEMENT OF SERVICE

3rd Squadron, 17th cavalry

Constituted 1 July 1916 in the Regular Army as Troop C, 17th Cavalry.

Organized 9 July 1916 at Fort Bliss, Texas

Inactivated 26 September 1921 at the Presidio of Monterey, California.

Disbanded 9 March 1951.

Reconstituted 1 March 1957 in the Regular Army and consolidated with the 11th Airborne Reconnaissance Company (active) and consolidated unit designated as Troop C, 17th Cavalry, an element of the 11th Airborne Division (later designated as the 11th Air assault Division.)

Relieved 1 July 1958 from assignment to the 11th Airborne Division.

Inactivated 15 November 1958 in Germany.

Activated 15 March 1962 at Fort Knox, Kentucky.

Inactivated 16 January 1963 at Fort Knox, Kentucky.

Redesignated 1 February 1963 as Headquarters and Headquarters Troop, 3rd Squadron, 17th Cavalry, and remained assigned to the 11th Air Assault Division (organic elements concurrently constituted.)

(Troop B, 3rd Squadron, 17th Cavalry, activated 7 February 1963 at Fort Rucker, Alabama.)

Squadron (less Troop B) activated 19 March 1964 at Fort Benning, Georgia.

Relieved 30 June 1965 from assignment to the 11th Air Assault Division.

Inactivated 1 July 1965 at Fork Benning, Georgia.

Activated 25 November 1966 at Fort Knox, Kentucky

Inactivated 19 June 1973 at Fort Lewis, Washington.

Assigned 2 June 1988 to the 10th Mountain Division and activated at Fort Drum, New York.

b. CAMPAIGN PARTICIPATION CREDIT

WORLD WAR II

Northern France

Rhineland

* North Apennines

Central Europe

* Po Valley

VIETNAM

* Counteroffensive, Phase III

* Tet Counteroffensive

* Counteroffensive, Phase IV

* Counteroffensive, Phase V

* Counteroffensive, Phase VI

* Summer - Fall 1969

* Winter - Spring 1970

* Sanctuary Counteroffensive

* Counteroffensive, Phase VII

* Consolidation I

* Consolidation II

* Cease - Fire

DESERT STORM - Restore Hope

BOSNIA

AFGHANISTAN

c. UNIT DECORATION

* Republic of Viet Nam Cross of Gallantry with Palm, Streamer embroidered VIET NAM 1967 - 1968

Republic of Viet Nam Cross of Gallantry with Palm, Streamer embroidered VIET NAM 1969 - 1970

* Republic of Viet Nam Civil Action Honor Medal, First Class, Streamer embroidered VIET NAM 1969 - 1970

* Valorous Unit Award, Streamer embroidered CAMBODIA (May - June 1970)

* Republic of Viet Nam Cross of Gallantry with Palm, Streamer embroiderd VIET NAM 1971

Republic of Viet Nam Cross of Gallantry with Palm, Streamer embroidered VIET NAM 1971 - 1972

* Joint Meritorious Unit Award, Streamer embroidered RESTORE HOPE (Dec. 1992 - May 1993)

d. 3/17 UNIT TRAINING HISTORY AND MOVEMENT TO VIET NAM

With the large build up of United States Forces in South Vietnam, there was a dire need for rapid and accurate gathering of intelligence for the field commander. To meet this need the 3rd Armor Squadron, 17th Air Cavalry Regiment was activated on 25 November 1966, at Fort Knox, Kentucky.

During the next two months before sufficient personnel were available to organize the Squadron into troops, the assigned personnel were kept busy ferrying the aircraft from the Bell Helicopter Plant in Fort Worth, Texas, to Godman Army Airfield at Fort Knox.

It was not until late January 1967 that the Squadron began assigning personnel to their respective troops.

On 26 February 1967, the Advanced Individual Training (AIT) phase of training began.

Each troop was given the responsibility of conducting a portion of AIT. A Troop was responsible for the Scout Observer

Training. Additional committee type training was given by the troop on the use of the 106mm recoilless rifle.

On 8 May 1967, the troop began Basic Unit Training (BUT). The exercises were conducted at Camp Atterbury, Indiana, and at the Mountain Ranger Camp at Dahlonega, Georgia. This afforded the troop its first opportunity to set up the Tactical Operations Center (TOC) and iron out some of its minor problems. This phase of training also gave the Troop's young aviators a chance to operate in mountainous terrain.

On 3 July 1967, the troop entered Advance Unit Training and moved to Camp Dawson, West Virginia. The West Virginia National Guard and the staff at Camp Dawson combined elements to act as aggressor forces during part of the training period. During this phase the troop underwent its Advanced Tactical Training to include displacement of the Command Post (CP) and Tactical Operations Center (TOC).

From 2 August through 4 August the Troop took part in the Squadron Advanced Tactical Training (ATT). It was administered by the U. S. Army Aviation Group (Prov) from Fort Knox. The area was used along the Green River Campbellsville, Kentucky.

The ATT covered all aspects of the Squadron's operations with emphasis placed on the activities of the Squadron and Troop Command Posts. Upon completion of the ATT the Squadron was declared combat ready.

The period from 5 August to 7 October saw predeployment Army Security Inspections (ASI), Command Maintenance and Material Inspections (CMMI). Preparation for Overseas Replacement / Preparation for Overseas Movement (POR / POM) qualifications and the final preparations for the movement to Vietnam.

On October 1967, the Troop departed CONUS by ship. The advanced party arrived Di An, Republic of Vietnam on 14 October 1967, and started preparation for the main body which arrived at Di An on 2 November 1967. During the majority of the days in November the troop was involved in in - country training, building a base camp at Di An, and basically becoming operational. During the period of activation from 25 November

1966 to 7 October 1967 and from 2 November 1967 until 30 November 1967 there were 355 days of training, 25 days of troop movement, and 31 operational days.

e. D TROOP HISTORY NOV. 1967 - NOV. 1968

The history of D Troop was a classic military example of the versatility of a ground cavalry reconnaissance troop. The troop performed a wide variety of missions due to its high level of training and aggressiveness. It complemented the mission of the supported unit. The troop performed in a dismounted role in the jungles as infantry. To Maintain the units versatile capabilities it continued to train in areas it was not being used so that it would be ready to take on any one or a number of its capabilities in support of the fast and changing situations of combat. The Blue Tigers were always proud of their accomplishments and were ready to go where the action was to do their job.

DI AN Troop D arrived in Viet Nam 2 November,1967 and began an intensive incountry training program located at Di An, Viet Nam.

FSPB HANOVER Troop D assigned to a 1st Infantry Unit December 1 - 4. Perimeter guard and ambush patrols.

SOUI DA On 7 December 1967, Troop D had the mission of escorting all 3rd squadron 17th Air Cavalry wheel vehicles into war zone C, and securing and defending a FSPB at Soui Da. During this period of time

Troop D conducted mounted and dismounted patrols, air mobile operations, convoy escorts, road clearing operations, and night ambushes.

TAY NINH On 5 January 1968, Troop D moved to Tay Ninh with the mission to conduct reconnaissance in force missions to the North and West of Tay Ninh.

FSPB On 19 January 1968, Troop D was detached from 3rd squadron, 17th Air Cavalry and placed OPCON to the 1st Battalion, 5th Infantry and conducted a tactical road march to FSPB 15 km North of Tay Ninh. Troop D's mission while at this FSPB, was to conduct mounted and dismounted operations and platoon size ambushes.

FSPB BURKE On 23 January 1968, Troop D moved to FSPB Burke located 9 km North of Soui Da. Troop D's mission was to provide security for an artillery unit of the 25th Infantry Division. While at FSPB Burke, Troop D again conducted dismounted patrols and night ambushes.

FSPB On 25 January 1968, Troop D moved to a new FSPB located on the East side of Nui Ba Den Mountain. From that location, D Troop conducted mounted sweeps to the Northeast of Highway 26 and conducted ambushes at night.

PREK KLOK On 9 February 1968, Troop D became OPCON to the 2nd Battalion, 34th Armor and conducted a tactical road march to a new forward fighting location at Prek Klok. Troop D's mission was to clear the 25th Infantry Division MSR from French Fort to Katum and escort supply convoys.

TAY NINH On 17 February 1968, Troop D was released from the 2nd Battalion 34th Armor back to operational control of the 3rd Squadron, 17th Air Cavalry. Troop D moved to Tay Ninh to build a new basecamp.

GO DAU HA On 25 February 1968, Troop D had the mission to sweep and secure the 25th Infantry Division MSR from Tay Ninh to Go Dau Hau.

TRANG BANG On 7 March 1968, Troop D became OPCON to the 4th Battalion, 23rd Infantry and moved to a FSPB located at Trang Bang, with the mission to sweep the 25th Infantry Division MSR from Trang Bang to Tay Ninh and secure the Trang Bang bridge.

PHUOC VINH On 20 June1968, Troop D became OPCON to Company F, 51st Infantry (LRRP) and moved by air to Phuoc Vinh as a reaction force for the LRRPs when in contact.

BIEN HOA On 26 June 1968, Troop D moved to Bien Hoa with the mission of reaction force for the 51st Infantry (LRRP).

FORT TIGER On 19 July 1968, Troop D moved to FSPB Fort Tiger while the mission continued as reaction force for the 51st Infantry (LRRP).

LONG BIEN On 21 July 1968, Troop D conducted a move to an artillery basecamp located East of Long Binh.

CU CHI On 12 August 1968, Troop D moved to Cu Chi for reaction force with the 51st Infantry (LRRP).

BIEN HOA October 1968, Troop D continued to support Company D, 151st Infantry,

(LRRP), as an airmobile reaction force in War Zone D. The troop also conducted special missions for Bien Hoa basecamp area in the form of mounted and dismounted reconnaissance and ambush patrols.

Kenneth D. Williams

About The Author

He was born in Guymon, Oklahoma in November 1944. As a boy, his family moved around a lot. But two places in his young life stands out as contributing to his love for writing. Ulysses, Kansas is where he attended junior high school, and Dumas, Texas is where he graduated from high school. He attended Oklahoma University for a short time. He received his BA in 1970 from Oklahoma Panhandle State University in Goodwell, Oklahoma. He received his MA Degree in 1972 from Western New Mexico University in Silver City, New Mexico. He also did graduate work at East Texas State University at Commerce, Texas in 1978. He has had many poems published beginning in high school. He has written many unpublished works to date. He served fourteen months as a combat infantryman in Vietnam - 1967-1968.

Printed in the United States
944900001B

9 781403 391926